LISA ENGLAND

Time Tangle

...ve she
... And
...vinced
...unning
... to be
...rheated

But wh... ...peared in the Tudor pavilion in th... grounds, looking for his hawk, she really was convinced she had gone back four hundred years to Elizabethan times. And when Adam asked her to give a crucial message to a fugitive priest to save him from capture by the Queen's men and almost certain death, Beth eagerly agreed—not telling Adam she was in a 'time tangle' between past and present. Then, on Christmas Eve, everything went terribly wrong. All Beth knew for certain was that she was in the Infirmary with a broken leg, and a terrible feeling of despair that she had let Adam down. Perhaps she had imagined the whole thing after all? Or had she...?

Girls of 11 and over will like this a lot.

TIME TANGLE

Frances Eagar

A Hippo Book
Scholastic Publications Limited
London

Scholastic Publications Ltd,
161 Fulham Road, London SW3 6SW, England

Scholastic Book Services,
50 West 44th Street, New York, 10036, NY, USA

Scholastic Tab Publications Ltd,
123 Newkirk Road, Richmond Hill, Ontario L4C 3G5
Canada

H J Ashton Co Pty Ltd, Box 579,
Gosford, New South Wales, Australia

H J Ashton Co Pty Ltd,
9–11 Fairfax Avenue, Penrose, Auckland, New Zealand

First published by Hamish Hamilton
Children's Books Ltd 1976
Published by Scholastic Publications Ltd 1980

Typeset by Computacomp (UK) Ltd, Fort William,
Scotland
Made and printed in the U.S.A.
Set in Plantin

Contents

'does time encircle us,
do words we spoke yesterday,
last week, last year, remain forever,
never lost, pressing all about us as day
by day we become our past?'

Willie Jones

One

Beginning at the End

I WAS SITTING up in bed when Dad arrived, propped against a huge pile of starchy pillows. I heard him crunching down the polished passage, not at all subdued by being right inside a convent.

'How is she?' he asked Sister Anne, the Infirmarian, but did not wait for a reply. He breezed through the door, all sunburnt and purposeful. He came to a sudden stop at the end of my bed.

'Hullo Beth,' he said, letting his airport bag plonk to the ground.

'Hullo,' I replied, rather startled to see him in the flesh after so many months of letters and telegrams. I had not realised that anything would make Dad come dashing back to England. Perhaps I was iller than I thought.

Perhaps at any minute now a solemn procession of black robed nuns would follow him into the room, lighted candles ready, to stand chanting round my bed while I, whiter than the sheets on which I lay ...

'Everything OK?' asked Dad cheerfully, breaking into my death bed scene.

'Everything except me,' I told him.

'Oh, yes!' He looked down at the cradle, humping the bedclothes over my leg. 'But you'll be up and about in a day or two. That's what the doctor said.'

The school doctor. A beefy, red man, like a slab of rump steak in spectacles. I could just imagine what he had been telling my father. For a change, I did not even need to imagine. I had heard him talking to Sister Anne just outside my door.

'Accidents are not always accidental, Sister,' he said cheerfully. 'Elizabeth is an unusually fanciful child. If you want my opinion, the whole drama is the product of an overheated imagination.'

'But the broken leg?'

Sister Anne could not agree that it was the product of an overheated imagination. I warmed to her.

'Oh, I'm not saying she did it on purpose. Just that it would not have happened to anyone else. You may even find it has done her good. Brought her up sharp to face reality, as you might say.' He laughed beefily.

I lay with my eyes half closed, ready to forgive him with a small patient smile, if he should look through the door. But he did not do so. He prescribed a bottle of mixed pills and squelched heavily down the passage. That was last night. I supposed that Dad must have telephoned him from the airport to get the lowdown.

I had almost forgotten Dad, still standing at the end of the bed. He looked sort of deflated and worried. As if he'd come to the end of his conversation, as well as his journey. I wanted to help him, but I could not think of anything to say.

'Look, Beth.'

Dad sat down suddenly on the end of my bed, just missing the broken leg. 'I don't know what you've been up to, and at the moment I don't suppose you feel like telling me.' I nodded. In fact, even if I wanted to tell him, I did not know where to begin. There did not seem to be a beginning and anyway I was still in the middle.

He fished around inside his airline bag and brought out a bunch of grapes and a fat rainbow-coloured notebook. He put them down on the bedside table and walked over to the window.

'What a view,' he said, pressing his nose to the glass. 'Look at it. Snow covered old England. If you don't count the water tower, there's nothing to tell you that you aren't in Tudor times.'

'Nothing at all,' I agreed.

Dad turned round, his hands in his pockets, and looked at me with his head on one side.

'We've been through it a bit this last year, Beth. I don't know what to do. I wish I did not have to work abroad because in some ways I don't think I'm the best sort of father for you.'

'Yes you are,' I said quickly. He looked crumpled. I did not know that grown-ups ever had those kind of thoughts. Suddenly I felt mean and selfish, to land up with a broken leg, bringing him rushing back from the Middle East so fast. He did not take any notice of my loyal interruption, but helped himself to the grapes and chewed a few thoughtfully.

'I'll tell you something that has always helped me. Whenever I'm really in a tangle and can't see the way out, I just start writing about it. I write it all down.'

'Is that what the notebook is for?' I picked it up and riffled through its glossy pages.

'Yes. You'll have to spend quite a time resting that trotter of yours, so you might as well have a try. Write it all down. You can always tear it up afterwards. But it really helps.'

It seemed a good idea. I wondered where I would begin. Probably with the telegram.

After Dad had gone I finished the grapes, tried to scratch my knee where it was itching under the plaster, then picked up the fat notebook. First the title. *Gone With The Wind.* No, that's already been used. Anyway, it was nothing to do with wind, more like echoes. *Wild Echoes Flying.* That sort of thing.

I closed my eyes and saw the bookshop, with row upon row of books. All mine. The school doctor, pale for once, with admiration.

'Elizabeth my dear, fanciful or not, I must say that reading your book has changed my entire life. Will you sign this for me?'

'Certainly,' I murmured, just before he vanished and I was left alone with the empty pages.

Perhaps the doctor was right. I have got an overheated imagination. Perhaps I'll never know if it really happened. But I'll put it down straight, just as it was, beginning at the bit where I was pretending to make a film because packing is so boring.

Two

The Telegram

'ACTION!' cried the director.

The cameras whirred. I strode across the room in glorious technicolour, filmed for the waiting millions. I could see them in red plush rows, gazing up at the screen out of the warm darkness, forgetting their drab everyday lives.

I pulled open a drawer and tossed a couple of exotic garments on to the bed. They fell into the suitcase neatly folded. That always happens in films. Packing is so easy. The cupboard door fought me for a bit. I yanked at it so that the whole cupboard danced up and down on its wormeaten legs. (Not quite the way it is done on the best Hollywood sets, but never mind.) An elegant evening gown, shimmering like the Milky Way, was tossed on top of the exotic garments.

Washing things. They never seem to need them in films, toothbrushes and things like that. I leaned against the basin and stared at myself in the glass, peering through the curtain of thick brown hair. Not bad. Good teeth and a nose that might one day be OK. A bit snub and freckly at the minute though. I wrinkled it and made a rabbit face. Mrs Flopsy Bunny. It must be very hard work chewing dandelions when you have to keep your nose twitching up and down. No wonder rabbits often looked so muddled. But this would never do. Actresses did not stop in the middle of films to make rabbit faces at themselves. I was the heroine, packing to leave because...

'Cut!' yelled the director, just in time, clasping his podgy hands in excitement. 'Elizabeth, you were great! Fantastic!'

The door crashed open. A large girl stood framed on the threshold. Even through the toothpaste spots and scratches on the flyblown glass, I saw that she was bursting with important tidings. But I was playing it cool. I swung slowly round, still leaning on the basin.

'You're wanted downstairs. I think it is about a telegram. A man came up the avenue on a red motorbike and gave a telegram to the Head.'

The director, the film star, the Hollywood set, faded into the mists. My stomach tightened and I swallowed hard. Telegrams, telegrams. For the hundredth time I wished that we lived somewhere in England. That Dad was not always being posted from one trouble spot to another, living in hotel bedrooms, typing out his chunk for the newspaper and queueing for the telephone to cable his office in Fleet Street.

When Mum was alive we'd had a home in England. Well, a sort of home, a cottage that we lived in when Dad was back on leave. Usually it was let to strange people who forgot to forward letters and feed the cat. But we'd sold it in the summer, cat and all. Dad hadn't wanted to live there any more. Come to think of it, nor had I.

Of course it was quite exciting, having a father who was always abroad. He wrote often; long letters about what it was going to be like in the Christmas holidays. The letters were handed out every day after lunch, by a spottily important prefect who liked to do it as slowly as possible, savouring every moment of her power.

'One for you, Elizabeth,' she said regretfully, when she could hide the truth no longer.

We usually took our letters to the cloakrooms and read bits of them aloud, as we hopped about changing for games. It was fun, to be able to tell the others what Dad said about Christmas picnics under the palm trees and camel rides by moonlight. Especially when I knew most of them were going to spend the holidays under a sodden English sky. It was mean of me, I know. But anyway they all had homes with lots of brothers and sisters and cats, and things like that.

'Hey, wake up, Beth! Didn't you hear what I said? You're wanted downstairs. A telegram.'

There I was, dreaming again. I thanked the girl and started for the door, my stomach bunched with dread. The longer I put off going downstairs, the longer I did not know what the telegram was going to say. Sometimes it is better not to know. Before you know, everything is all right, and then suddenly afterwards nothing can make it the same again.

It was like that in the summer term, after the car crash. One moment everything was just normal, and afterwards engulfingly terrible. Every morning I woke up with that awful feeling you have after a nightmare; but every morning I realised that the nightmare was still there. It was like swimming through a black sea, very slowly and quite alone, over one giant wave after another. It was no good hurrying. It was no good asking for help; the black waves were part of my life and only I could do the swimming.

But the telegram was probably only about the plane; after all Dad couldn't ring up. Perhaps they'd changed the time of the flight. Anyway, it was better to find out. I thanked the messenger and started down the corridor, weaving in and out of the trunks that stood, locked and roped, awaiting collection.

The staircase is wide and highly polished. I had to walk down it slowly, step by step. We were forbidden to run, ever since Cathy had tripped on the shallow steps and gone straight through the mullioned window on the half landing. She'd crashed on to the roof of the bicycle shed, with only a scraped shin and the most astonished face I have ever seen. No real harm was done, except to the Tudor glass, of course. The lead frame had bulged and exploded outwards, scattering hundreds of diamond shaped panes into the courtyard below.

'Glass,' as the Headmistress told the school in the chilling voice she used for these occasions, 'glass that has withstood the attentions of Oliver Cromwell and Adolf Hitler, smashed by a careless child.'

There they were, Cromwell and Hitler, arm in arm, regardless of the centuries that separated them. They were throwing pebbles up at the Tudor window. It was dark and they were locked out. Cromwell's collar and Hitler's face gleamed pale in the moonlight. When would someone hear them? Would they have to throw pebbles all night?

I had reached the bottom of the stairs. A throng of girls, waiting for the school bus to take them to the station, milled about in their coats and berets. There was an expectant hush gathered round the door of the Head's study. It sounds peculiar, but that is what I saw. They too had heard the red motorbike and rumours of a telegram. They wanted some drama to while away the last few hours of term. I pushed through them and knocked on the study door.

'Come in.'

Crossing that threshold always makes my knees feel as if they have had an electric shock. It did then, even though I knew I was as innocent as driven slush, or whatever the saying is.

The Headmistress sat enthroned behind her desk, her round pink face framed in the white coif and dark veil. She smiled at me and I knew at once that the telegram was not just about a change of flight.

'Elizabeth, my dear, I'm afraid I have a great disappointment for you. Your father says you cannot join him for Christmas.' She looked down at the telegram in her hand and continued.

'With the new trouble in the Middle East, he is working day and night. He says it would be no holiday for either of you, as he would have no time to look after you.'

I stared at the ground. The floorboards merged and swayed before my eyes. Rage, (yes, I think it was rage) swirled inside me so that I almost overbalanced. I scowled fiercely at the blurred floorboards. I knew I was expected to say something.

'If only, if only,' I said, and my voice sounded

small and strangled. 'If only he wrote about water rats or football or parliament, then we could live in England.'

The Head came round her desk and put her arm on my shoulders. Like all the nuns, she smelled comfortingly of soap and starched linen.

'I know it is hard,' she said gently. 'But he must be every bit as disappointed as you. You are all he has now, and I know how much you mean to him.'

There was another silence. I swallowed and glared at the floor.

'Let's look on the bright side, my dear,' she continued. 'He will come home as soon as he can. And at least we will be able to hear that lovely voice of yours, singing the Christmas carols.'

A lump in my throat swelled, tight and hard as a fist. I did not feel I could ever sing again. I nodded, mumbled something, then turned and walked out of the room.

The throng were there, but I pushed through them. Usually I would have played the film star game. 'No comment,' I would have told them, while flash bulbs exploded all round. Dark glasses concealing my feelings, I would have stepped into the waiting limousine and been swept away to... to wherever it was.

But I pushed through them, hating them all for going home. I ran across the hall and down the wide tiled passage. My ribs ached and squirmed inside me.

'Beth—'

I heard Cathy call behind me, but I ran on, faster and faster, crashing through the swing doors at the far end, and into the gritty solitude of the cloakroom.

Alone among the deserted games boots and the sickly smell of oiled lacrosse sticks, I tried to breathe slowly and carefully. Then I saw my orange scarf, dangling from a peg. I remembered the cottage, cat and all. I remembered last Christmas.

'You stupid fool!' I said angrily, but it was no good. The sobs burst out, huge and suffocating, as if they had been wanting to come for a long time. If anyone had come in, even Cathy, I think I would have murdered them.

Three

The Far Side

'WE THREE KINGS of Orient are',

Sister Emmanuel sang as she gathered the sheets and pillowcases and flung them into a waiting basket.

> 'One on a bicycle, one in a car.
> One on a scooter, blowing a hooter,
> Following yonder star.'

'Sister Emmanuel!' I was shocked. I did not know that nuns sang such irreverent songs.

'What's the matter, dear?' she said dreamily, her arms full of crumpled sheets. I sang the verse again and we both laughed.

'The words must have floated into my head when I was helping with the little ones,' she explained. 'That is the way it happens with songs. You sometimes don't even know where you have heard them.'

'I know that feeling,' I said. 'You have something that has drifted into your head and it is the only thing you can sing, and you are quite fed up with it, then it suddenly goes away.'

'You'll be singing for us this Christmas, I hope,' said Sister Emmanuel. 'Mother Christina told me how much she is looking forward to hearing your voice.'

'I'd love to,' I said, thinking of the frail old nun who was Reverend Mother before the war. None of us had ever seen her, but she knew all about us, and sent each single person a card on their birthday. I wanted to sing for her.

'I'll do the song I sang in the pageant, and wear the lovely green velvet dress.'

Then I blushed and felt all hot and prickly. It had sounded so swollen-headed, so I busied myself in the far corner of the dormitory.

We did a pageant in the summer; a play about all the famous people who had lived at Belvedere. I was Anne Boleyn, in a bottle-green velvet dress made of some old curtains, with silk-lined sleeves. I had to sing Greensleeves, that Henry VIII had written especially for his new queen. It was all very unnerving. I nearly died of fright.

But this voice of mine, I've no idea where it came from. I'm not really swollen-headed about it. Our singing teacher tells me it is a gift from God. But I don't know why it picked on me. Mum never sang a note and as for Dad, he sounds like a raven with a sore throat. But I have got this voice. Dad says it reminds him of plum brandy and it does sound peculiar coming out of skinny me. I'm not the right shape for my voice. I should be a pear shape, standing on its stalk, with a magnificent bosom for diamonds to sparkle on. I'm more the shape of a stick of celery. Still there is always hope.

My job was going down the long line of wash-basins in the dormitory, collecting all the scraps of soap and dropping them into a bucket. It was already half full of scraps from the other dormitories, as we had spent the whole afternoon clearing up. This was obviously the sort of thing that happened at the end of every term.

'What do you do with all these little bits of soap?' I asked Sister Emmanuel.

'We melt them and make them into new bars. Nothing is wasted here.'

A soap factory. White-coated attendants hurtling up and down with stainless steel trolleys. Steam hissing and scalding as a pink waterfall of boiling soap cascaded down the cooling tower, was channelled into moulds, cut into chunks, sliced, wrapped, packed, rushed on to the conveyor belt. I stood by, my hand on the lever which worked the emergency generator; ready at a moment's notice to... What do they do with emergency generators anyway?

'Perhaps you can help,' said Sister Emmanuel, as she fought with the straps of the laundry basket. 'We've got to find something for you to do until your father comes home.'

That was it. There was nothing to do. There wasn't a home to go to either. I breathed gloomily on the window and drew a face in the mist. I often breathe on windows when there is absolutely nothing to do. It makes them rather smudgy, but it helps to pass the time.

Beyond the mist I saw the dark woods, hunched behind the tall Tudor chimneys. The water tower on its spindly black legs looked especially bleak and miserable, like the watch tower of a prisoner of war camp.

I saw a film once. The prisoners planned an escape. They tunnelled out of their hut and came up beyond the barbed wire, in the tufted grass between the wire and the woods. They had hoped the tunnel would come up under the cover of trees. But the searchlights picked them out, as they scuttled like rabbits for the safety of the dark woods. One got away. He was caught later by the dogs. The worst thing would be the waiting, I thought. Waiting to be captured.

'Daydreams, daydreams,' said Sister Emmanuel in my ear. She looked at me with her penetrating blue eyes. 'I do believe you spend half your life in the clouds; most of this term anyway.'

'What else is there to do?' I was really feeling very sorry for myself.

'Well for a start,' she said in her no-nonsense voice, 'you can move house.'

I like Sister Emmanuel. She hasn't been a nun that long and some of the oldest girls can remember her before she became one. There is a rumour that she had a motorbike and went all round America on it. She is good fun, in a teasing sort of way, and a real help. She even taught me how to waltz.

The fiercely corseted lady who teaches us ballroom dancing said I could not attend another lesson until I had mastered the 'art of the waltz'. I did not want to attend one anyway, but it seemed I had no choice. Sort of 'heads I win, tails you lose'. But Sister Emmanuel offered to help and we clumped round the cloakroom, twisting our ankles on scattered lacrosse boots, while she intoned:

'Forward, side together, side!
Back, side together, forward!'

After one lesson she said I waltzed like an army on manoeuvres. But it was a waltz.

'Come on,' said Sister Emmanuel, 'pack your suitcase.'

I looked at my bed, with the half packed suitcase still lying on it, clothes heaped where I had left them that morning, when the telegram came.

'But where am I going?'

The school was empty. The trunks were gone and the last of the girls had left for home.

'You'll have to come over to our side and stay in one of the guest rooms.'

'Over to your side!'

I was astonished. I pressed my nose to the window again and stared across the gravelled courtyard to where the far wing of the Tudor house loomed out of the twilight. Although I had spent eighteen months as a boarder at Belvedere, I had never yet set foot past the Chapel that divides the great house like the central bar of an E.

Beyond the Chapel is the Enclosure, where the nuns live. They live here from the day that they first enter the convent to the day that they die. Some of them come over to the School side and teach, or play games or run the laundry. They go to museums and conferences, and drive the school bus, and are ordinary mortals. But some of them live on the far side all the time and are only seen gliding through the Wilderness, as the bleak wood is called. We are not allowed in the Wilderness as it is part of the Enclosure, but I'll tell you more about that later.

I had often wondered what lay behind the far Chapel door. In the summer nights, after we had finished our usual diversions and were too wide-awake to go to sleep, Cathy and I used to look across the courtyard to the bow windows of the far side and tell each other stories of girls who had ventured across and were never seen again. Though of course their pale faces were sometimes glimpsed at a window, as they wasted away in solitude.

The far side was as fascinating for me, Cathy and most of the others, as the darkest corners of Soviet Russia. Secret and remote. Yet there was Sister Emmanuel calmly inviting me to spend Christmas there. I turned round to stare at her, unable to believe my ears.

She laughed.

'Don't look so startled, Beth! Anyone would think you're going to spend Christmas on the moon. Come on, finish your packing. I'll carry the suitcase.'

We left the dormitory and walked down the long, echoing corridors, turning off lights as we went. Gradually, the whole school side of the house became dark and dead. The only light I could see was at the very far end of the Chapel passage. Breathless with excitement, I followed Sister Emmanuel into the far side.

* * *

'But it is all so ordinary and old!' I was rather disappointed, but too polite to say so.

'What did you think it would be like?'

Sister Emmanuel turned round, halfway up a spiral staircase that led out of a huge oak panelled room.

'I thought it would be...' I closed my eyes, searching for words to explain what I had imagined. My mind teemed with shadowy halls, hung with velvet that was black and soft as the night, pinpointed by candle light, wreathed in incense, with monotonous chanting, tolling bells, holy and remote.

A smell of new bread wafted up the stairs and Satan, the convent labrador, trotted by on his way to supper. I gave up.

'Just different,' I said lamely, unable to begin.

'You see, this side of the house was not bombed in the Second World War,' said Sister Emmanuel. 'Most of the School side had to be rebuilt because it was damaged by bombs.'

'By bombs or by Cathy,' I said, thinking of the mullioned window on the main staircase.

'Yes, poor Cathy!'

Sister Emmanuel laughed at the memory. 'But tell me, Beth,' she continued, eyeing me shrewdly. 'You did not see much of Cathy this term, did you? I thought you two were such friends.'

'I did not see much of anyone,' I said, and hoped that would end the conversation.

It is not that I don't like Cathy. I do. For the first year I was here, she was my closest friend. She even came back to the cottage with me for the summer half-term, not long before the car crash. But ever since then I just feel she is trying to be kind. I can't explain it. I can't explain to anyone how fierce and sad I feel inside. It seems easier to bury it and pretend to be someone else. I suppose that's why I spend my time daydreaming. It makes things seem less real and when they are not so real, they can't hurt so much.

Anyway, the far side was real; and it was

exciting. I followed Sister Emmanuel, telling myself that I had just entered the convent, with all my bright young life behind me. The doors had closed. I had tasted my last ice lolly. Ahead of me lay years of rising at dawn, night after night of sleeping on bare boards in a narrow, draughty cell.

We climbed another flight of stairs. We were really getting under the rafters. I wondered if the cells had bars on their windows. No, that was the wrong kind of cell. It would be bleak though, with a little hard bed, a cross on the wall and no other ornaments.

'Look, this is your room, Beth. You're not too far away from anyone. This is the nearest guest room to our cells.'

'Thank you,' I said and she glided away, her sandals squeaking on the bare boards.

I looked round my little room. It was definitely not a cell. It was nicer than anything I had ever imagined. It was painted duck egg blue, small and very high ceilinged, almost as if it were a bite taken out of a bigger, grander room. There was a low divan, with a flowery cover like the ones in the sixth form bedsitters. The cupboard was new and shiny, far more suitable for a Hollywood film set than the wormeaten one in the dormitory.

I lay back on the bed and rejoiced in the comforts of a squashy mattress. Around the ceiling and dotted about the walls were little Tudor roses. They were so painted over that their shapes were almost obliterated. They were not arranged in any special pattern; just glued on here and there, as if they had been put in their proper places but had slithered down the wall when the plasterer had gone to bed. One had even snaked its way down to floor level and squidged against the oak boards.

Those roses really cheered me up. They made long ago, over four hundred years ago, seem so much nearer when I knew that a plasterer could make a silly mistake like that.

If I closed my eyes, I could see him in front of me, a jolly round figure, dressed in homespun brown clothes, his plump face smooth with astonishment when he saw what had happened to his fine plasterwork.

'Lookee, Dickon, what has thou done to yon pesky flowers?' the master plasterer said. 'The King's Grace will not like to see his great Tudor roses slithering down the walls like by-our-lady snails.'

Dickon gaped and I gaped too. Neither of us could think of anything to say.

But what had King Henry said, when he saw the walls of his new palace of Belvedere? Had he come round on a good day, when he was jolly and laughing, with Anne Boleyn on his arm? Or had he come round when he was feeling mean and angry, with shifty red eyes and a short temper? Poor Dickon (or whoever he was) I hoped the King had been kind to him. But then I decided that it was probably such an unimportant little room that the King had never climbed up to it at all and never knew that his Tudor roses had behaved like by-our-lady snails.

I unpacked my clothes and put them in the chest of drawers. There was hardly a thing that fitted me, except my school uniform which I would rather die than wear in the holidays. I had two pairs of jeans, a horribly frilly ballroom dancing dress that was much too tight and a couple of jerseys. I don't suppose Dad had thought about clothes for the holidays. He's not very good at that sort of thing. He's not very good at decorating either. When we were painting the cottage, he had just the same sort of trouble as poor Dickon.

I laughed as I lay on the squashy mattress and remembered Dad painting the bathroom ceiling. He had lost his balance, trying to perch on the hot tap and paint the farthest corner. He had fallen full length into the bath, with the can of paint on top of him.

We had to turn the cold water on and Dad sat in the bath, clothes and all, using the most colourful language, while the paint was washed away. He said he had never realised that painting was so dangerous and Mum had told him that painters did not usually balance on the bathroom tap, like the statue of Eros in Piccadilly.

Then I stopped. Whatever happened, I was not going to think about the cottage. I looked at the slithery roses and they made me laugh again. That decided me. I knew what I would think about. Long, long ago. I suppose that was really the beginning of the tangle.

Four

Wild Echoes Flying

IT WAS TWO days later that I received a letter from Cathy. I found it when I was wandering listlessly round the hall, trailing my fingers along the radiators and reading the faded names on the Honours Board.

The envelope was lying on the doormat and as I saw my name I felt the usual rush of excitement I always get, even when I know exactly how boring a letter is going to be. Sometimes I fill in hundreds of little coupons in the Saturday papers and for weeks am peppered with important brown envelopes full of sample hearing aids and brochures offering me peach trees whose fruit will grow at an amazing rate and stun all my friends.

'Dear Beth,' Cathy wrote on her parents' poshest writing paper.

'My mother was very sorry to hear that your holiday plans have been cancelled and hopes that you will come and stay with us.'

I looked at the letter. It was written in Cathy's best writing. The sort she used for an essay called 'What I did with my holidays' at the beginning of each term when she was still feeling keen. Next term she would be able to write:

'In the holidays I asked Elizabeth Lorimer to stay because my mother told me to.'

It was a put up job. I was sure of that. Cathy never used words like 'your holiday plans have been cancelled.' It was Cathy's mother. If I closed my eyes I could see her, standing over Cathy and telling her what to write.

Cathy's mother is a brisk and terrifying woman, about the shape and size of a pillar box. She wears scarlet suits and is a Juvenile Magistrate. She has X-Ray eyes, barely concealed behind flashing blue spectacles. I am scared of her.

I stood holding the letter until I heard the swish of long skirts coming down the passage towards the hall. Then I suddenly crumpled it up and stuffed it in my pocket. It seemed the best thing to do. If I wrote and said 'No, I can't come,' Cathy's feelings would be hurt because she would know it was not true. If I wrote and said 'Thank you, I would love to come,' that would be worse because I would have to go and stay with them. All I really wanted to do was spend a dreamy time by myself, drifting about the place.

In fact I hardly had any time for daydreaming; the nuns seemed determined to keep me as busy as possible. After we had tidied upstairs, we started on the classrooms.

'I never thought there was so much work to be done in the holidays,' I said, as I sat with Sister Columba in the little bookroom that afternoon, helping her sort the textbooks.

'What did you think happened?' Sister Columba looked up from a dog-eared copy of *Hamlet*. She was painstakingly gluing together all the chunks that had fallen out after a term's rough handling by the O Level year.

'I thought it would be different.'

I did not want to confess that I had always half imagined Belvedere frozen into a sleeping beauty trance where absolutely nothing happened until the first girls returned and the spell was broken. But the nuns were as busy in the holidays as in the term time. The only difference was when the great bell rang for Divine Office and the nuns went to Chapel.

Then a pounding silence enveloped the school. I sat with my ears straining, trying not to listen, and heard curious pistol shots that sounded like a distant revolution. At first I thought they were machine gunning the Chapel.

Hundreds of parachutists had floated down and seized the place. I was going to be martyred. I hoped it would all be over quickly. Long-drawn out martyrdoms were much worse and you were not even anything more special at the end of them.

They would put up a statue of me. A pink and white plaster one, with a sheaf of lilies in my hands and my eyes rolling up to the heavens and 'Blessed Elizabeth Lorimer' inscribed on the pedestal, 'who died in an odour of sanctity'.

'Girls!'

Reverend Mother's voice trembled with emotion. 'I want you all to try and model your lives on this shining example...' Oh yes, in some ways martyrdom would be very satisfying. Later I discovered it was not machine guns, only the hot water pipes in the ancient central heating system.

Sometimes I went to the Chapel and listened to the nuns chanting plainsong. But at other times I liked to wander around and just enjoy the emptiness of Belvedere in the holidays. That way it belonged to me. But this was all too complicated to explain to Sister Columba and sounded too much like nonsense. She is very down to earth. So I picked up the top book from the pile I was supposed to be cleaning and started work with my rubber. The ink blots became black and fluffy if I rubbed them, but the pencil doodles came off without a struggle. I read a faint scribble, already half rubbed out, written in the large round hand of a first former.

'England, Europe, the Northern Hemisphere, Planet Earth, the Solar System, The Universe, Space,' I read aloud. 'I wonder why people write that sort of drivel in their books.'

'Boredom, I suppose,' said Sister Columba, as she put the newly repaired *Hamlet* back on the shelves.

I knew why when I thought about it. It is those long dull afternoons, when tea time seems an eternity away and Friday will never come.

There was the interstellar postman, dressed in flowing silver plastic, like a space age angel, floating through the blackness of outer space. He was returning the book to the address which the creature from Planet Earth had so thoughtfully written on the flyleaf. Below the address the creature from Planet Earth had added:

'If you have to learn a poem, try page 86. Lots of it is the same.'

I am no culture vulture, but there was nothing better to do. I flipped over the pages to examine page 86. It was a good tip. The last two lines of each verse were more or less the same. I read them aloud.

'Blow, bugle, blow, set the wild echoes flying.
Blow bugle; answer echoes, dying, dying, dying.'

'Tennyson,' said Sister Columba. 'He is always so mournful.'

I wandered over to the window, repeating the words inside my head.

'Where do echoes go to?' I asked, balancing on the hot water pipe that ran along the skirting board. Not only echoes, I thought, but all sounds. If they were like ripples on a pond, they must go on and on, getting fainter and fainter, but still there.

The bell started to ring, from the belfry above the Chapel. A solid, monotonous tolling. I imagined its notes, swelling out in ever widening circles, beyond the enclosed garden, beyond the bare trees of the Wilderness, across the fields towards the village, then on and on, getting fainter all the time, but still there.

'But where do echoes go?' I turned round from the window.

'I don't know, but I'm going to Chapel.'

Sister Columba untied the check apron that she wore over her long black skirt. She smiled at me as she picked up her prayer book.

'What you want is a hobby to help you pass the time, Beth. Remember that after Vespers we go straight into supper.'

I listened to the swishing sound as she retreated down the polished passage, towards the Chapel corridor and the far side.

The bell had stopped. A huge silence descended. But the interstellar postman, if he had the right sort of ears, would still be able to hear those echoes, or anyway those sounds, travelling towards him. If he could hear sounds that left the earth long ago, perhaps he could see long ago too. After all, light travels in waves as well as sound.

I looked up into the wintry sky. Somewhere, millions of miles into space, it would be possible to see light waves that left Planet Earth more than a thousand years ago. Perhaps on some far away star, there lived a race of intelligent beings who could sort them out with a special telescope. They could look down and see the Roman Forum at the height of Rome's power and not know that starving cats now stalked each other through what was once the centre of the world. (I saw the starving cats in the summer holidays and gave nearly all my lunch to them. Dad said it was just as cruel to feed them, as I could not do it every day, but they were so hungry.)

But this race of intelligent beings on the far away star might even now be looking down on Belvedere and seeing all the trumpets and fanfare of King Henry's Court. Or later, when it belonged to a chap called Sir Jocelyn Something and Queen Elizabeth made one of her visits. That must all be somewhere, getting fainter and fainter, but there just the same. What if something happened in space, a huge explosion that sent the echoes of long ago rolling back again? Then those light waves would mingle with waves from things we see around us today. It was perfectly possible. I looked nervously round the little bookroom, imagining fat Sir Jocelyn fussing over the last minute arrangements for a royal visit.

The doorbell rang. A loud electric buzz. I

woke out of my daydream with a crash. I hurried through the darkened hall; no time to grope for light switches, and pulled open the heavy studded door. The postman stood on the doorstep, stamping with cold, a woollen scarf wound several times round his neck.

'No lights on,' he said, 'and all so quiet. When I heard your footsteps I thought you must be a ghost.'

'Well I'm not,' I said feebly, as I took the letters from him. None of them was for me, but I was not really expecting one. I'd had my letter for the day, and it was scrumpled in my pocket.

'Better luck tomorrow,' said the postman kindly. 'You here for the holidays then?'

'Yes.'

I stood there awkwardly, not knowing what to say. It was not the most brilliant conversation of my life but the postman looked tired and cold and his breath made sad little puffs in the wintry air. It was all gloomy and dank, and the gloom and dankness settled inside me. Three days of the holidays had passed and already it felt like light years. I had to find something to do, but everything I could think of seemed pointless. All I really wanted to do was go home to last Christmas.

The red mail van dwindled down the avenue until it faded into the late afternoon murk. In a plantation beyond the enclosure wall, two men were felling Christmas trees. I heard the whine of their saw and watched them carry another little tree and load it on to the trailer. The tractor chugged a few yards. It looked no bigger than a toy and the men were little black pins, hardly different from the tree they were carrying.

Just out of nowhere, a thought floated into my head.

'The postman thought I was a ghost. I wonder if they would think I was a ghost too?'

Five

The Grey Lady of Belvedere

IT WAS NOT one of my best ideas. Written down, in cold blood, it looks rather silly. But I was feeling depressed and badly in need of something to do.

At first I tried pretending to be a novice, with all my bright young life behind me. But that was impossible. My room was so pretty with its slithery roses, that I could not turn it into a narrow cell. At night I imagined I was lying on bare boards with just one hairy horsehair blanket on top of me, but the mattress was the squashiest thing I had slept on for months. So even in the dark, it did not work.

There was the bathroom of course. That was bleak enough to be a narrow cell and quite good for practising being a hermit. But even the most hygienic hermit cannot prolong his bath for more than an hour. In fact, I was not sure if hermits ever bothered about baths. All those huge oil paintings of hairy hermits fighting off temptation never look as if they considered cleanliness was next to godliness.

Mealtimes really were strange and the nearest I could get to pretending I was a nun. We ate in silence, while one of the nuns sat in a sort of pulpit and read aloud from some improving book.

If anyone was late, they had to cross the vast acres of polished boards and bow to Reverend Mother, who is very tall and so pale that she does not seem to be made of flesh and blood like ordinary mortals. She is surrounded by an aura of majesty and on the rare occasions when I am late for meals, it takes as much courage to walk to her table as it would to mount the scaffold on Tower Green.

I knew Cathy would be very envious when she heard about my meals; but even then when I looked around the room there was usually a friendly face to smile and make sure that I was not feeling too lonely. And the sight of the cheerful novices soon squashed any ideas I might have had about pale faces wasting away at windows. So there I was, really on the far side, but unable to make it exciting.

But as I stood in the doorway looking across the courtyard in the late afternoon murk, there was nothing to show that this was here and now. Only the water tower looked out of place. I shut my eyes firmly and imagined Belvedere in Tudor times.

'I'll drift across the courtyard,' I decided, 'and glide through the woods near the tractor, hardly seeming to touch the ground.'

I threw the letters on the table inside the door and was poised for take off when I noticed my clothes. Ghosts do not wear jeans and jerseys; not yet anyway. (In another century or so there will probably be hordes of them, just as many as all the knights in armour who roam about these days.) I wondered if I could borrow one of the nuns' cloaks. As they had all taken a vow of poverty, nothing belonged to them, so in a sort of way it would be all right. There was one. I could see its dark shape through the mottled glass in the door of the Head's study. But even in the holidays I did not feel up to crossing that threshold of my own free will. Also I remembered that although nuns made excellent ghosts in most places, one more at Belvedere would not startle anybody.

Then I remembered the clothes for the school pageant. They were stored in a room built under the stage, at one end of the assembly hall. I ran down the passage. There was no time to lose, as the nuns were probably halfway through Vespers.

The room was musty and dramatic. It smelt of greasepaint, which always makes me think of first nights, and telegrams and lots of crackly bouquets of flowers and strange people kissing each other and saying 'Darling, you were divine!' But there was no time for a triumphant first night. I pushed away the cheering fans and turned on the light.

The Archangel Gabriel's robe was still dangling from a hanger by the door, left over from the end of term Nativity Play. A pair of wings, whose crepe feathers were graded from pale primrose to deep flame, were folded on a chair beside it. Just for a moment I had a vision of myself appearing before the men as they worked in the fields, splitting the air with a 'Gloria in Excelsis'. That would be even more startling than a ghost. But then I remembered that angels flew.

I pulled out a suit of chain mail, made from knitted string sprayed silver. A Norman knight? I struggled into the top half. It had no glamour. I looked more like a knitted twit. Then I saw my own dress, that I had worn as Anne Boleyn in the summer pageant. In a way it was mine and I really wanted to wear it again. But it was flimsy and the neckline was too low for a soggy winter evening. Yet Tudor was obviously the best thing to be. I imagined Anne Boleyn throwing something on over her dress before nipping out to fetch her lute that she had left in the rose garden. A cloak. I found one and pulled it out. It was grey velvet, the soft silver grey of willow leaves. I tried it on and felt like the Lady of Shalott, withdrawn and anguished, pale and remote.

'The Grey Lady of Belvedere.'

That was what they would call me, once they had got over the shock, of course. The cloak had a huge silver clasp and a fur-lined hood that was really most becoming. With the hood well down, I felt ready to haunt anyone, even Reverend Mother, without fear of recognition.

All the same, it was nerve-racking crossing the courtyard. At any moment I felt a window would open and a voice call out:

'Elizabeth! What on earth are you doing?'

The back of my neck felt prickly. I had left it a bit late. But I was afraid they would finish cutting the Christmas trees that day because there was only a week to go until Christmas. Then there would be no one left to haunt.

In fact haunting is a very difficult business, full of technical hitches. I had always imagined ghosts just glided by filling everyone with fear, but it did not work like that. It is impossible to fill people with fear unless they have noticed they are being haunted. I began to wonder just how many poor ghosts trail up and down, wringing their hands while no one bothers to see them. Perhaps we only see what we expect to see. Perhaps we have to be specially tuned in to see ghosts, even pretend ones.

I crossed the bumpy, sodden lacrosse pitch and walked up beside the chicken run where I had spent so many fruitful hours hypnotising hens while not defending my goal. (In later life I expect I will be glad of these hypnotic powers I am developing; they will be far more useful than lacrosse.) The plantation was on the far side of the Enclosure wall, just by the edge of the Wilderness. I slipped through the gateway and walked slowly along the outside of the mellow brick wall, skirting the edge of the Christmas trees. But the men never stopped to look fearfully around in case a ghost should come gliding out between the dark trees. Or a wolf, its yellow eyes gleaming.

Did wolves leap silently from behind? Sinking their teeth into their victim's throat before she had a chance to cry out. Or did they howl first? A long mournful howl, like something out of a Russian winter, that gave the victim a chance to run for the safety of the tractor. Perhaps wolves were not afraid of tractors.

'There are no wolves in England,' I said aloud, to discourage any that might be slinking behind me. I immediately switched to thinking about vampire bats. They flew. They could cross the Channel from Ruritania or wherever they lived. Sunset was their favourite time for gliding about with staring eyes and pointed white teeth. Once they had sunk their teeth into their victim he (or in my case, she) was doomed. Night after night they returned until their grisly work was done. Eminent physicians were summoned, but none of them knew the cause of the mystery illness that drained me of my life's blood. Day by day I became weaker and paler until...

It was time to stop this morbid train of thought. I pulled the ruff of the cloak tightly round my neck and left the shelter of the trees. The newly cut stumps dragged at my cloak, but I managed to move smoothly enough, giving a fair imitation of a ghost.

'Good evening, Sister,' said one of the men politely as I crossed his path.

'Good evening,' said the ghost and glided hastily through the gateway.

What a flop! Most things work out like that if you stop to think about it. The hens tittered and cackled scornfully as I leaned against the netting of their run. The Grey Lady of Belvedere bared her teeth at the hens and considered her next course of action.

In the house, great squares of light flashed on. Vespers were over. I had left it too late. I did not want to meet anyone as I crept in the front door. I was already feeling a big enough fool for one day. The best thing would be to hide the cloak and come back and fetch it quietly the next day. I undid the clasp and looked round for somewhere to leave it.

It would be out of the rain in the hen house, but the hens were watching and nudging each other; probably longing for a chance to sabotage the cloak in revenge for all the times that I had hypnotised them. A hollow tree? But I did not know how to tell which ones were hollow. I stared at the dark elm trees on the edge of the Wilderness. They all looked equally solid or hollow. It might take hours to find the right one. Then I remembered the pavilion.

On one of those endless afternoons of last summer, when we were supposed to be playing tennis but our balls and rackets had mysteriously become stranded on the spreading branches of the cedar tree, Cathy and I had come up to the edge of the Wilderness and were tempted by its leafy shade. We crept silently in, as wary as soldiers in occupied territory. It was the very first time I had put a foot in the Enclosure and I was uneasy.

'What is a Papal Bull?' I asked.

'Oh, it's nothing dangerous!' said Cathy airily. She is a Catholic and should know about these things, so we crept further in through the ferns.

After padding down an overgrown path, we came to a tiny clearing where the grass grew long and juicy and butterflies hovered above the stems of cow parsley. In the middle of the cow parsley, shimmering in the heat of that drowsy afternoon, was a little house. It was built of the same apricot bricks as Belvedere and was six sided, with a pointed, mossy roof.

'Just look at that!' I whispered.

'Do you think it was the Royal Privy?'

'Of course not!' I said quickly. 'Too far from the house.' (Cathy always has dreadful ideas like that, when I am ready to imagine an enchanted castle.)

'I think it is what they called a pavilion,' I

said. 'I expect Henry VIII used to come here when he wanted to get away from the cares of state. He used to sit strumming on his lute practising a new duet!'

'All by himself?' Cathy turned to look at me. 'Rather a funny duet!'

We began to laugh, then suddenly a twig snapped. Someone was walking along the path. Perhaps it was one of the mysterious nuns from the far side, one of the ones we had never seen before. We melted back into the ferns and fled the forbidden wood.

But now I had spent two days on the far side. I no longer feared that a Papal Bull would come snorting after me if I went into the Wilderness, its mad eyes red as a Cardinal's hat. Besides, I wanted to explore the pavilion while I was certain that everyone was in the house.

It was difficult to believe that the sodden little track was the same one we had followed in the summer. The ferns were russet brown and trampled by the rain and brambles strayed across the path, dragging at my cloak. Above my head the black branches dripped sadly. The sky seemed to press down on them, cold and unrelenting. I thought of a poem I had read last term.

> 'A widow bird sat mourning for her love
> Upon a wintry bough;
> The frozen wind crept on above,
> The freezing stream below.'

Apart from the freezing stream, the place was exactly right. I looked up at the lifeless branches and half expected to hear the song of the widow bird.

It was also horrifyingly quiet. The kind of silence that pounds in your ears and you feel is full of eyes. I knew I was crazy to come to the Wilderness at dusk and that if I stopped to think about it, I would never reach the pavilion at all. It was time for the emergency plan to swing into action. Elizabeth was scared, so she became someone else. The widow bird.

I was the Lady Imelda, mourning for my lost love. He had ridden down the avenue to fight the Saracen, a year last Michaelmas, and still no word had come of him. Had his ship been captured by Barbary pirates? Perhaps at this very moment he was chained to an oar in one of the galleys that plied up and down the Mediterranean. The overseer, twirling his cruel moustache, raised his whip in the air.

'Alack the heavy day!'

I covered my face with my hands. The cloak fell off. I suddenly felt all unprotected. I picked it up and ran towards the clearing.

The pavilion was still there. I had half expected it to have been a summer dream. No one but Cathy and I knew of its existence and we might almost have imagined it. But it stood in the twilight, surrounded by yellowed leaves and the bare stalks of last summer's cow parsley. The panelled door was covered in frilly grey lichen. As I pushed it open, it scraped across the tiled floor, making a horror film noise. This was almost the last straw. My heart thumped and I was ready to turn and run. But I swallowed hard and steadied myself. I had not come so far to be put off by spooky noises.

It was shadowy inside, a sort of cathedral

gloom and cold. I shivered and pulled the cloak around my shoulders again. There was a drift of long dead leaves across the floor and as the cloak swept through them they crackled like cornflakes. Above my head the rafters arched to a central blob in the roof. I peered up at it and could just make out the dusty outline of a Tudor Rose.

Then it really was King Henry's pavilion! I knew it. It was just the sort of place a king needed to forget his troubles. A hideout where he could pretend to be a simple charcoal burner with no more worries than where the next meal was coming from. I was sorry that King Henry was not a little more romantic. He was so fat and dreadful. But perhaps deep down inside he knew how repulsive he was and that must have made him feel worse than ever.

There were diamond-paned windows set into five of the walls and the sixth was the door. I sat down on one of the window seats and thought how much I should like to come back another day, perhaps every day of the holidays. No one would know where I was. I could do whatever I liked. This was my house.

I pressed my nose to the mossy glass. Outside the Wilderness was waiting. A crow cawed bleakly as it flew home to bed. I felt the shivers coming on again. But Anne Boleyn would not have been scared of a wood on a winter evening. She was tough. Even on the day of her execution she had chatted and joked with her jailers.

'Queen Anne Boleyn,' I said aloud and saw before me the dark girl with the slanting eyes, who had been King Henry's Queen for so short a time. Then I looked up into the rafters and sang her song. I sang it so the roof rang with noise.

'For Greensleeves was all my joy,
And oh, Greensleeves was my delight,
Greensleeves was my heart of gold ...'

Then I stopped. I remember this clearly. Whatever people say, I remember stopping, because even though my voice was filling the little pavilion with sound, I knew there was something behind it.

It was not an echo. It was more than an echo. Echoes do not give you back what you have not sung and I have never sung like that in my life.

The sounds died away. I stood frozen in panic, not daring to look round the dusky room.

Six

A Voice in the Wilderness

I DON'T KNOW how long I stood like that. It felt like an age. Everything was suspended in a sort of icy horror. There was something there and that something had sung. I could not have finished the last line if my life had depended on it. I opened my mouth and a bullfrog croak came out. I was as sure as I have ever been of anything that a voice had soared high above my own. I was sure it was not an echo. But I was also not sure as well. I was afraid that my imagination had at last taken control and I was starting to hear Voices, like Joan of Arc.

But as I stood in that musty pavilion, all I really heard was the painful thump of my own heart as it crashed up and down like a yoyo in my rib cage. Then softly, just when I was beginning to feel that I really had imagined it, I heard the last line of the song.

'And who but my lady Greensleeves.'

The sounds died away. This time I was certain it was not me. I would have bet a hundred pounds to a blood orange that someone was behind me and I knew I was going to have to turn round and find out who it was. Ignoring the shiver that was crawling up and down under my cloak, I swung slowly round.

My first thought was relief that he was real. I don't know what I had been expecting, but it certainly was not an ordinary boy, sitting hunched on the window seat. His face was a pale oval in the dusk, topped by dark hair. The rest of him melted into the shadows. He was looking straight at me.

My second thought was a tidal wave of embarrassment that he had been a silent witness to my performance. Help! What had I been doing and saying? Why did words always flow in such a torrent from my mouth? He probably knew all about Lady Imelda and the Barbary pirates, not to mention Anne Boleyn. What a fool he must think I was! For once, I was quite bereft of speech.

'That is an old song.'

He smiled, but in a friendly way. Well, if he had joined in he could not think it was all that crazy. Perhaps lots of people go round singing in sodden woods at twilight. But if he had laughed, I think I would have rushed out and slammed the door and that way I would never have found out any more about him.

'It is a very beautiful song as well,' I heard my voice say, rather shaky and thin, as if I was an extremely old lady. Then my knees gave way. I think it was what first aid handbooks call delayed shock. I sat down suddenly on the window seat, facing him across the little room. The yoyo was settling down in my rib cage, but I was still not up to small talk.

He locked at me. He seemed to be considering me carefully.

'Do you live there?' he asked, waving his hand in the direction of Belvedere.

'Yes, I do.'

Once I had started speaking, the words flew out in a rush of relief. 'I'm staying there for Christmas. My father lives abroad and I have no home in this country; not since my mother died last summer.'

Then I stopped. I was angry with myself for starting to tell this boy my life history. It was nothing to do with him and would only lead to a long and awkward silence. I've noticed this. When people hear about Mum they get very embarrassed and I can see them trying not to mention mothers. They are as careful as if they are walking on eggs; it is much worse for both of us that way. But this boy did not look embarrassed.

'I am truly sorry,' he said quietly.

'I don't want to talk about it!'

I stood up and paced briskly through the leaves scattered on the floor.

'Yes, it is hard,' I heard him say, through the crunching of the leaves. 'It is hard to accept the death of those whom we love.'

'Hard!'

I swung round in the middle of my pacing. How did he know what he was talking about! You rage inside, you despair, but just to accept that you will never see someone again!

'It is not just hard, it is impossible!' I said angrily.

'There is no other way!' His voice was equally fierce. 'There is no other way to be able to go on living.'

I stared at him. His nostrils were pinched, his blue eyes flashed. No one had ever talked to me like that. Suddenly I felt as if I was the one who was walking on eggs. I fumbled with the clasp of my cloak.

'Anyway, what are you doing here!' I said as haughtily as possible. 'These woods are private.'

If the Wilderness was forbidden to me, who came from Belvedere, it was surely even more forbidden to him.

He leaned back against the wall and smiled cheerfully.

'I've come to look for my hawk,' he said.

'Your hawk!'

This was like a conversation in *Alice in Wonderland*. I did not know which way we would be going next.

'Yes, she flew into these trees and I followed her.'

'Well, you don't seem to be looking very hard.'

It was all I could think of to say.

'Oh, it is much too late now. She will have settled in a tree until sunrise. I will ride over early tomorrow and lure her back when she is hungry.'

'Ride over! What on?'

'A horse! Did you think I would ride a pig?' He laughed aloud. I flushed angrily and turned to look out of the window. The woods seemed thicker and blacker than ever, but there was no sign of a horse anchored to the dripping trees.

'If you had a horse, I would have heard you trotting up the avenue,' I said suspiciously.

'Oh, I did not trot up the avenue like a fine gentleman out hunting,' he laughed. 'That is not my way. I rode by the fields from Darnbury and came quietly through the back of the woods.'

'So that's where you live.'

I know Darnbury. It is about eight miles away on the far side of the valley, beyond the motorway. On clear summer evenings the church tower sticks up out of the woolly trees and it looks like a toytown village. I looked back at the boy again. He did not seem at all conscience-stricken about trespassing in the Wilderness, an interloper in my pavilion. He was smiling as if enjoying a secret joke, as if he was laughing at me.

Suddenly I knew why. He had been in the woods all the time. He had probably seen my failed attempt to haunt the Christmas tree plantation and heard me being the Lady Imelda and wringing my hands. Now he was enjoying the game, pretending he was something out of the Middle Ages, with his hawk and his horse. In another minute he was going to inquire after the health of the Barbary pirates. I shook with a mixture of shame and rage.

'You need not think you can make a fool of me!'

I drew my cloak about me, ready to sweep out of the door.

'Please believe me. I am not mocking you!'

He jumped off the seat, all trace of laughter gone. It was then that I noticed his clothes.

He was dressed in black, from head to foot, except for a white shirt open at the neck and a silver chain that gleamed inside the collar. His clothes were muddy and stained with lichen, as though he really had been scrambling through the trees after his hawk. A short cloak swung from his shoulders and his hose was torn at the knee. This strange boy, who I had believed to be mocking me, was dressed in the clothes of four hundred years ago.

I stared at him; my mind whirled, unable to take in what I saw. He leaned forward and took hold of my hands, his face sharp with concern.

'What is the matter?'

'It is nothing.'

I did not know what to say. He was dressed in strange clothes, but then so was I. Had he been playing some game like me, or what? His clothes looked so comfortable and everyday, as if they were part of him. And he looked so ordinary. That was the most confusing part of all.

'What is your name?'

'Adam Martin,' he said, stepping back and bowing slightly. A perfectly ordinary name. We stood facing each other in the silence. He seemed puzzled, unable to understand what was worrying me.

'And what is your name?'

'Elizabeth,' I said mechanically. And then from far away, beyond the trees, I heard the thin tolling of the Chapel bell and I remembered the time. Six o'clock—the hour of the Angelus.

I pulled open the door. 'I must go.'

'Shall I see you again?'

His face was anxious. It seemed very important to him. He is lonely too, I remember thinking. He needs a friend as much as I do, and for a moment I almost liked him.

'I'll come tomorrow,' I said, 'and help you search for your hawk.'

'Oh yes! That will be hard to find!'

He laughed and once again I had the feeling

that there was some secret joke; that he was mocking me.

'That is a game that two can play,' I said aloud and I turned and ran from the pavilion.

The Angelus was still ringing as I crashed headlong down the sodden path, a hundred thoughts whirling like a blizzard in my head. But uppermost, the size of a snowball, was the dreadful thought of having to walk the whole length of the silent refectory and apologise to Reverend Mother for being late for supper.

Seven

The Priest's Hole

THERE IS A RULE at Belvedere that you stop whatever you are doing when the Angelus bell rings. You stop and you say the prayers. At first I had not known what to say, but I soon picked up the words from the others. But I was not stopping this time, not for anyone.

I hurtled headlong down the side of the chicken run and back across the lacrosse pitch. It was lucky I knew the way for it was pretty dark and I had to watch where I was putting my feet. I did not want to trip over a molehill and cover the velvet cloak in mud. I was watching the ground so carefully that I never even noticed Father Lewis until I ran slap into him.

We reeled together and swayed to and fro; me clutching him round the waist, he grabbing the air for his breviary which had been catapulted out of his hands. Then at last we settled down on an even keel again.

'Someone is in a hurry!'

Father Lewis smiled at me as he readjusted his gold-rimmed spectacles.

'Yes, I'm late for supper.'

I paused to catch my breath, before running on again.

'I'll have to walk into the refectory all alone,

with everyone watching. Oh how I wish they talked at meals!'

'Well, come and have supper with me,' said Father Lewis, 'Sister Agnes always brings me enough for two and as you can see I hardly need fattening up.'

He smiled modestly down at his rounded cassock. I laughed. There is a rumour at Belvedere that Father Lewis and the cedar tree have the same vital statistics, but no one has ever got round to proving it.

Not that he was always so round and healthy. Ages ago, when he was a pale young missionary, he had been taken ill in the tropics with a sinister disease and sent home to England to die. He had become chaplain at Belvedere to while away the last few months of his tragic life. And here he is, half a century later, round and jolly and loved by everyone. Only one symptom remains of his sinister disease. Mosquitoes absolutely refuse to bite him.

This is very hard on the rest of us. On summer evenings he likes to walk slowly round the grounds and it is lovely to walk with him and ask him all about Belvedere and who lived there long ago. He always knows all the answers, but he stops by the boggiest bits of ground to talk about it. And we squirm and wriggle in a grey cloud of insects while he stands calmly in our midst, quite unbitten. But that night was far too cold for mosquitoes, so I was happy to walk back through the dusk with him.

'I'm sure Sister Emmanuel will be worrying about me,' I said.

'We'll send a message by Sister Agnes. She'll know you can't be far away.'

'I've had the fright of my life in the Wilderness,' I began and then stopped. The pavilion was in the Wilderness and the Wilderness was part of the Enclosure. I was sure that Father Lewis, like everyone else at Belvedere, would forbid me to go there. Although I really like burbling away about everything, I realised I was going to have to keep the pavilion under my hat. The nuns used the Wilderness for silent meditation and would not want to know that I was creeping round it in a grey velvet cloak.

'The cloak!' I said suddenly, realising that I was still wearing it. 'Oh dear, what shall I do?'

'Now you just stop fussing about everything and come and warm your toes at my fireside.'

Father Lewis does not use the main school door, nor the convent one. He had his own little blue door tucked in a courtyard round the back. There was no one to see me come in, no one to notice I was wearing the cloak. If I had planned it, I could not have managed it better.

'We'll just hang your coat up here,' said Father Lewis, hooking it on a peg beside his own black greatcoat. He was far too vague to notice how glamorous it was. He had not noticed that I had rocketed out of the Wilderness either. I thought he was wonderful to be so dreamy. It gave me an idea.

'May I always leave my cloak here, Father?' I asked politely.

'Why yes, of course, if you want to.'

There it was. As easy as that. I could collect the cloak and go back to the pavilion again any time I felt like it. No one would ever know.

'Make yourself at home,' said Father Lewis,

as he led the way into his little sitting room.

The room was whitewashed, with a polished floor. In one corner a carved crucifix was nailed to the wall, with a prie-dieu below it. There were books heaped on every flat surface and in tottery piles in all the corners. In front of the fire were two red plush armchairs, so bursting with stuffing that they looked as if they would explode if anyone sat on them. I lowered myself gingerly on to a swollen surface and watched Father Lewis fill his pipe. The whole place smelt rough and different, quite unlike any other part of Belvedere. Hairy and rather like a cinema. The flames danced, yellow and gold, and I leaned back in my chair and stretched my toes towards the fender.

'What does it feel like, to be here alone in the holidays?' asked Father Lewis, looking at me over the top of a flaring match.

'Well, it is very interesting to be on the far side,' I told him. 'The others won't be able to believe their ears when I tell them.'

'Oh yes!' he chuckled to himself. 'The Secrets of the Far Side.'

'There are some,' I said. 'For instance, my room. I've never seen anything like it before. It has Tudor roses all over the walls and they have slithered around like snails and dried on just anywhere. No one could possibly imagine a room like that.'

'Oh, so that is where you are,' said Father Lewis. 'Well, I have a real secret for you; not that you'll be able to do much about it. I am pretty certain, from the archives in the library, that there was a priest's hole at Belvedere in

Elizabethan times. It may well have been in the Tudor rose room.'

'A priest's hole?'

I nearly fell into the fire in my excitement.

'Well, I'm not sure,' said Father Lewis modestly. 'But it seems more than likely. In the records of the day, they mention a carpenter called Nicholas Owen who worked here in 1592. You can see some of his panelling in the Chapel which was, of course, the banqueting hall in those days. Later, under Oliver Cromwell...'

'But the priest's hole?'

I prompted him gently. It was fatal to let Father Lewis escape into his favourite topic, Belvedere and the Civil War.

'Ah yes. Well it seems that by day Owen worked as an ordinary joiner, but at night he constructed hiding holes for the Jesuit priests in many great houses throughout the land. No two were alike, so that even if the Queen's men discovered one priest's hole, they had no clue as to how to find another. Some are known, but many more have been forgotten and are so cunningly hidden that they may well keep their secrets for ever.'

'But what makes you think there was one in my room?'

'The household accounts of the time mention that Owen worked on several odd jobs about the house, among them the fireplace in the Tudor rose room. But what I wonder,' said Father Lewis, sucking his pipe thoughtfully, 'was why he should want to do any work there at all. It is such an unimportant little room. We can see with our own eyes that the fireplace is Tudor, so he did nothing to change the style.'

'So perhaps he worked *behind* the fireplace,' I said slowly and I knew what I wanted to do for the rest of the holidays.

* * *

Father Lewis was right. Sister Agnes did bring him enough supper for two. But when she saw me, she went away and fetched a plate of ice cream and chocolate sauce as well.

'I don't have puddings,' Father Lewis told me. 'But it never seems to make any difference.'

'That's because we look after you so well, Father,' said Sister Agnes, her brown eyes twinkling. 'We can't have you fading away now, can we?'

'Not much chance of that,' said Father Lewis ruefully as he put the pudding down in front of me.

'Do you think any priests ever came to Belvedere, Father?' I asked, as we sat by the fire in a comfortable after supper doze.

'It is more than likely,' Father Lewis said, 'but only a handful of people would have known about it; not Sir Jocelyn of course, but there may have been many in his household who still secretly belonged to the old faith. The rest of them would never even have suspected the man was a priest.'

'Did they have lots of different disguises?'

'Oh yes, all sorts. A real ragbag of disguises. Everything from clowns to courtiers. There was one priest, Father John Gerard, who might easily have come here, for he spent much of his time working in these parts.'

'What was he like?'

I wanted to be able to imagine the person who

might have hidden in the priest's hole that might be somewhere near my room.

'Oh he was a fine fellow,' said Father Lewis, chuckling to himself. 'He was so merry and full of tricks that not even some of his closest friends knew he was a man of God. Sometimes he used to ride about on a horse, disguised as a country gentleman, asking if anyone had seen his hawk. That way he got himself invited into many great houses. Once Father Gerard was in the house, he would work to bring the Catholics the comforts of their religion.'

'But did he really have a hawk?'

I leaned forward in my chair. The answer seemed very important.

'Of course not!' chuckled Father Lewis. 'That was the best bit about it.'

I thought of Adam in the pavilion. I remembered his face when I had said I would come and help him search for his hawk.

'Oh yes! That will be hard to find!' he had said, with a carefree laugh.

Suddenly my head felt like a tumble drier. There were far too many things whirling around inside it. I sat in the overstuffed armchair trying to unravel them. I could hardly believe that three hours ago I had been trailing round the house wishing something interesting would happen. Now I did not know where to begin.

'Of course, in the end it made no difference,' Father Lewis was saying. 'The country never went back to the old faith and about three hundred men were martyred for a lost cause. But they died gloriously, for what they believed to be the truth.'

'Thank you very much for the supper,' I said, getting unsteadily to my feet. I was afraid that if I stayed any longer I would start talking about the pavilion and cosy though Father Lewis was, I was sure he would take the same side as a Papal Bull when it came to breaking the rule of the Enclosure.

As I lay in bed that night, I wondered what it was like to be hunted like a fox across your own homeland; never secure, never knowing from where the betrayal was going to come. Knowing that in the end the priest hunters were bound to capture you. There were more of them. The odds were on their side.

Suddenly, perhaps in one of the houses where the priest felt most secure, the Queen's men would arrive. They would thump about, banging the panelling with their staves, shouting to each other, forgetting in the excitement of their chase that their quarry was a man and not a beast. Then a panel would ring hollow and they would splinter it open and find him, helpless as a rat in a trap. There was nothing for him to do but surrender with dignity and pray for courage in the long ordeal.

Perhaps in this very room, behind the fireplace, a priest had crouched in a dark and airless cupboard, praying for deliverance.

I was almost asleep before I thought of Adam. 'I'll go and see him tomorrow,' I remember saying, 'and find out what game he is playing.'

But the following morning, disaster struck.

Eight

Mrs Weston's Invitation

SEVEN THIRTY. The alarm clock ticked smugly on the bedside table. It knew I would soon have to get out of bed. I reached out a hand and turned its face to the wall. It really was freezing! The first savage cold of winter. This was a day for getting dressed in a warm cavern under the bedclothes. I decided to act fast, so I could have half an hour in bed to warm up before breakfast.

In a brief dash across the room, I scooped up my clothes and shoes and pounced back into bed. The cold air sliced through my pyjamas like a knife.

Outside in the passage I heard the swish of long skirts as the nuns returned from Chapel and walked silently towards their cells. In spite of their romantic lives I was glad I was not a nun; at least in the early mornings. I did not think I could manage to be in Chapel by six o'clock every morning.

I wondered what saint's name I would choose. Some of the early saints had quite extraordinary names that sounded like Italian cheeses.

'Sister Gorgonius,' I said and my breath made a puff in the air. It was much colder on the far side than in the school. But then I knew that nuns did not notice creature comforts. Their lives were full of self denial, no lolling on radiators or toasting their toes in front of roaring fires.

But there had been a fire in my room once, long ago. I looked at the fireplace. The sharp outlines of its carvings were blurred by four hundred years of paint. I remembered what Father Lewis had said the night before. Was it really true that the master carpenter Nicholas Owen had worked here by candlelight, while the rest of Belvedere slept, muffling his hammer blows as he built a hiding hole for Catholic priests? How many people in the house had known about it? How long would it take me to find it? I only had three weeks left of the holidays.

While I watched in the shadows, the fireplace seemed to swing slowly away from the wall. I closed my eyes...

There was a flight of narrow steps cut into the brickwork. I inched my way up it. The bricks scraped my hands and knees but I was unaware of the discomfort. The air was dank and dark and above me gleamed a square of light. I crawled towards it, disturbing the dust of the centuries. As I put my head and shoulders through the hatch, I saw I was level with the floorboards, in a wedge of room built under the roof. There was a small window, festooned with cobwebs, a window through which the morning sun shone steadily; a window that a thousand people had seen from the outside and never given it a second thought, yet no face had looked out from it for almost four hundred years...

Ratatat tat!

The door started to open. I almost broke the

world record for sitting high jump. I was certain the Queen's men had arrived.

Sister Emmanuel poked her head into the room.

'Time to get up—and I've got some news for you.'

'What's the matter?'

My heart was still thumping at my narrow escape from the priest hunters.

'Nothing is the matter, Beth—cheer up.'

She laughed at my startled face.

'I only looked in to tell you that Cathy's mother had invited you to stay. She had a long chat with Reverend Mother last night. She really wants you to spend Christmas with them.'

'Yes, I know, she ...'

I bit off the words, remembering the scrumpled letter I had stuffed into the pocket of my jeans.

'I don't want to go, I'm afraid.'

I hoped I sounded mature and firm. Old enough to make my own decisions.

'You must go, Beth. It is all arranged. Apparently Cathy wrote to you the first day of the holidays, but the letter is probably lost in the Christmas post. Mrs Weston will collect you this morning.'

'Just like a parcel!'

The words flew out before I had time to stop them. Sister Emmanuel gave a patient sigh and stepped into the room.

'Look, Beth. During the next few days we go into retreat, we do not talk at all and spend a great deal of time in Chapel. You would be very lonely. Reverend Mother agreed with Mrs Weston that you should have the companionship of someone your own age.'

'But I've got someone...'

Once again I stopped. I saw that I was going to lose the battle because I could not use any of my big guns. Adam, the house in the Wilderness, the priest's hole. It was all too private to talk about.

'It is just that I did want to spend Christmas here,' I said. 'If I can't be with Dad, it is the next best thing.'

'But you will be here for Christmas, Beth. We want you here, too. Don't forget that Mother Christina is longing to hear you sing! Now cheer up. You'll be back on Christmas Eve, unless you change your mind and decide to stay with Cathy after all.'

I was indignant. 'I wish I could change the next few days instead. Why do I have to be dumped in their house without being consulted. Oh why did that bossy woman have to invite me?'

'I trust that you will be both polite and helpful.' Sister Emmanuel's voice had changed and the new model stabbed the morning air like an icicle. She crossed the room and drew the curtains, twitching them briskly into place. They obeyed without a struggle.

'I know we are urged to mortify our flesh,' she continued with eyebrows raised. 'But do you have to sleep *on* your shoes?'

Game, set and match to Sister Emmanuel. She billowed from the room, closing the door softly behind her.

'Polite and helpful,' I repeated through clenched teeth.

I thought of Cathy. She was probably dreading my visit as much as I was. If I had never been her special friend, it would not have mattered. But I knew she did not understand why I had tried to avoid her. Well, I didn't either. It was all going to be dreadful.

'I wouldn't be lonely, anyway,' I told the door. 'Not now that I've met Adam.'

Adam. Great Heavens! I had forgotten all about him in the excitement of having a priest's hole to find. He had said he would be over at sunrise to search for his hawk. I rushed to the window. It was a frosty morning. The sun was a red disc above the rim of the wintry fields. It looked as though it had been there for ages. Perhaps Adam had come and gone. If he had gone, I might never see him again.

I flung on my clothes and hurtled out of the door. There was no one about; no one to see me as I scuttled along a rabbit warren of passages and stairs until I reached the courtyard by Father Lewis's flat. My cloak was still hanging where I had left it the night before. I did up the clasp as I ran out of his door and up the back way towards the Wilderness.

Why did I go to all the bother of fetching the cloak? I have wondered about that since, as I've lain in bed puzzling over the whole business. I did not stop to think about it at the time. I just knew that the cloak was right for the sort of person I wanted to be. Adam was mysterious. Well I would show him I could be mysterious too! I was not going to let him have all the fun.

The morning air made my cheeks tingle. I jumped the frost-spangled molehills that lay on the playing fields. In spite of Mrs Weston's invitation I felt glad to be alive and bursting with excitement.

On the edge of the Wilderness a few last yellow leaves clung tattered against a pinkish sky. I took a quick look round and then plunged into the wood.

The pavilion was empty. At first I did not believe it. I shut my eyes, took a deep breath and then looked again. It had never occurred to me that Adam would not be waiting. He had seemed to want to see me again. He had seemed lonely, as if he needed a friend. Then I thought he might be out in the wood, looking for his hawk. I walked into the clearing and stood in silence. How did people call hawks? Did they whistle or yell? There was no sound but the distant rumble of a train carrying commuters to London.

I went back to the pavilion and sat on the doorstep, my chin in my hands. Sunrise, Adam had said. That was probably an hour ago and I was far too late. The story of my life seemed to be like a series of balloons at a toddlers' Christmas party. Joy, excitement, colour and then BANG!! Down to earth. A limp rag.

But when I thought about it I realised that Adam had probably never bothered to come at all. If he really lived near Darnbury, he would have had to get up in the dark to reach Belvedere by sunrise. Even if he had a bicycle instead of a horse, it did not sound likely, not on a frosty morning.

The more I thought about it, the more I realised that Adam was lying warmly in bed thinking about the twit he had met the night before who was silly enough to believe his story about a hawk!

Well I was glad he would never know I had believed him. If I ever met him again (and that was not likely), I would certainly keep quiet about my morning dash. I would not give him a chance to feel smug. He'd looked quite smug enough already—smug and mysterious—making a fool of me.

Sunbeams slanted like searchlights through the tree trunks. Each branch, each twig and blade of grass was frosted white. All at once I was glad to have been up early enough to see it. The Wilderness was so perfect that it was almost unreal; like a Christmas card. All it needed was Good King Wenceslas and a few fat robins to complete the picture.

I took a deep cold breath and decided not to care about Adam and I sang jauntily to prove it to myself.

'In his master's steps he trod
Where the snow lay dinted...'

I shouted, marching round the back of the pavilion in case Adam was hiding there. He wasn't.

'Heat was in the very sod
Which the Saint had printed.'

I have often wondered how that poor over-worked little page, armed with flesh, wine and pine logs, managed to tread in his master's steps without falling flat on his face in the snow. Perhaps King Wenceslas was an unusually small man who minced along. He certainly did not help the page or carry his fair share. Perhaps royalty never carried picnic baskets.

'Page and monarch forth they went
Forth they went together
Through the rude wind's wild lament...'

It was no good. Even the rude wind did not cheer me up. Nothing could hide the sagging feeling I had inside me. I knew then just how much I had wanted to see Adam again. I stopped singing and aimed a kick at the heavy wooden door of the pavilion.

'Adam—I believed you. I thought you were a friend!'

'So you did come after all!'

The voice sounded softly, from inside the little house. I peered in, wondering if I was going off my rocker. But Adam was there, leaning against the window seat, looking smug as a Cheshire cat.

My big toe throbbed angrily. 'What are you doing?'

'I am looking for my hawk.'

'Oh you and your precious hawk!' I snorted. 'I will bet you haven't even got a hawk. You're only saying that because you stole the idea from... from...' But then my voice trailed away into a sheepish silence.

Adam's face had gone pale, a finger flew to his lips. His eyes begged me to stop talking. He came to the doorway and stood beside me in the sunlight.

'What talk is this?' he said softly.

'Oh, nothing,' I said, and then added 'anyway

why did you hide from me? What sort of fool do you think I am?'

'No sort of fool, Elizabeth. I wanted to be certain you were not followed.'

So he *was* being mysterious again. 'Not followed' indeed! This was real cloak and dagger stuff. But then as I looked at him I realised that he meant it. His face was tense and anxious. He was hollow-eyed as though he really *had* been up half the night. Whatever game he was playing at, I was pretty certain it was real to him. I had never met anyone else who did that before and I did not know quite how to react.

'Elizabeth,' he said thoughtfully. 'You share a name with our Sovereign Lady the Queen.'

It seemed rather a colourful way of putting it. I shrugged my shoulders, unable to think of a suitable reply. All this mystery had rather put me off my stroke. The Grey Lady of Belvedere was at a loss for words.

'What do you know of the man without a hawk?' he said at last, so softly that I hardly caught the words.

'Only that Master Owen prepared a place for him,' I heard myself reply and, before I knew what was happening, I was in it too deep to get out.

Nine

Te Deum Laudamus

AS SOON AS I had spoken, everything changed. The Wilderness seemed darker and thicker. The trees loomed closer, as though they were eavesdropping. For no reason at all, I felt a lurch of real fear; almost fear of Adam. He looked so intent and his eyes bored into me, searching my face until I was almost ready to blurt out some excuse to explain I was only joking. But I did not know where to start.

At last he shrugged his shoulders and his face relaxed into a friendly smile.

'Shall I tell you something, Elizabeth?' Now I was going to learn what all the mystery was about! I felt quite giddy with excitement.

'Yes, please do!'

'You have a beautiful voice.'

Plonk! I was let down as usual; and on top of that I never know what to say when complimented about my voice. I fiddled with the clasp of my cloak and muttered something about it being a gift of God.

'Then let me hear you sing the Te Deum.'

I blushed with horror. 'I shall feel such a fool! Anyway I cannot remember the words.'

'Try and remember them.'

He was not joking. It seemed very important

to him. I cleared my throat and began, feeling extremely foolish.

'Te Deum laudamus
te Dominum confitemur
te...'

I shook my head. 'It's no good. I cannot sing it without my missal.' He smiled.

'No matter. You sang enough of it for my purpose.'

He looked at me again, as if making up his mind about something momentous. Then he said 'I have prayed for help and I believe you are the answer to my prayer.'

My jaw dropped open. I shut it again fast. Not very becoming, but I was pretty startled. I had no idea what was coming next from this strange boy.

'For the past two days,' Adam continued, 'I have waited on the fringes of this wood, not daring to come closer to Belvedere in case I was seen, yet knowing that time was running out.'

'Why were you afraid to be seen?' I asked. He seemed to be overdoing the drama a bit.

'My family is forbidden to travel more than five miles from our home. It is the new law against the Catholics.'

He hesitated and then added 'We are known to be of the old faith, since Tom was taken in the summer.'

'Who is Tom?'

'He was my brother.'

Adam glanced down and fingered the silver chain that hung inside his shirt. He pulled out a chunky silver cross and held it so tight in his hand that his knuckles gleamed white. Suddenly I felt as if I were an intruder. I wanted to melt away and leave him with his thoughts. But I also wanted to stay.

Then he tucked the cross inside his shirt again and smiled.

'Well, if you cannot sing all the Te Deum, let us sing Greensleeves again. You shall be Queen Anne Boleyn as you were last night, and I shall be King Henry.'

I followed him into the pavilion. It seemed friendlier than before. A lute lay propped against the wall. I knew it was a lute as soon as I saw it, even though I had only seen them in paintings.

'I have kept this under the window seat,' he said. 'Then my father knows that I have practised a new tune and does not think that I am dawdling away my time.'

He played to himself, completely absorbed as if he were alone. It was a lilting carefree tune, quite unlike his mood of a moment ago. If I closed my eyes I could imagine leaping log fires, tapestried halls and ladies dancing with their lords. I wanted to dance as well. But I sat primly with my cloak wrapped about me, to show him that in spite of all appearances I was really rather sensible and did not deserve to be teased about Anne Boleyn, nor about anything else for that matter.

'Will you sing with me?' said Adam, playing the opening bars of Greensleeves. 'Say that you will, Mistress Boleyn!'

'If you like,' I said, my primness melting away. 'It is a pretty tune that you have composed, your Grace.'

'Pray think nothing of it, Madam,' laughed Adam with a courtly bow.

So we sang Greensleeves together; first straight through and then pealing out variations on the chorus until the pavilion vibrated with sound. We finished breathless and laughing. Adam was fun and he had a fantastic voice as well.

'Show me how to play the lute,' I said, taking hold of it.

'You do not know?' said Adam in surprise. 'I shall teach you, but it will take time.'

'Time! Oh goodness, I haven't got any time!' I said, suddenly remembering breakfast and the full horrors of being late.

Adam jumped up. 'I need your help,' he said and his face was anxious again.

I looked at him. I longed to say that I could help him. He was the most interesting person I had met in my whole life and I would have given my ears to be able to stay and find out more about his plans. But Mrs Weston's dreadful invitation flashed like a neon sign in my brain. I knew that I must tell him the truth.

'It is no good,' I said sadly. 'I cannot help you at all.'

'Why not, are you afraid?'

'Afraid!' I would have laughed if I had not felt so miserable. 'Of course I am not afraid. But I have to go away until Christmas Eve. I won't even be here.'

'Nor I, until Christmas Eve. It is on that night I must have help.'

I looked at him and a little flicker of cheerfulness flared inside me. Perhaps I could help after all.

'It is not only for me, Elizabeth. It is for someone else. Believe me, his freedom, perhaps his life, will be at risk if I cannot find someone we can safely trust. I shall be here at sunset on Christmas Eve. I shall wait for you, but I dare not wait too long or my father will send to know where I am.'

'I shall be here,' I said and I knew that I would manage it, even if I had to run the thirty miles or so back from the Westons' house.

Adam took hold of my hand, his face lit up in a cheerful smile.

'There is one thing you must do before we meet again.'

'What is it?'

'It is a secret.'

'Why so many mysteries?'

'Do not ask questions,' said Adam, 'but promise to tell no one what I am about to tell you.'

I was half dead with curiosity. I had to find out.

'Very well,' I said. 'I promise not to tell a single soul.'

'This is what you must do,' said Adam. 'Look at the stars!'

'What a stupid idea!' I felt cheated. 'The stars cannot possibly be a secret. The whole world can stand and look at them.'

'But not understand,' said Adam gravely. 'Look at the stars and find the Little Bear. That is all I shall tell you now, for your own sake.'

At the words 'for your own sake', a shiver curled slowly down my spine. I ignored it. I did not want Adam to see I was scared.

'Christmas Eve at sunset,' I said and ran from the pavilion. Everything about him was such a mixture. I did not know if he was making a fool of me or if the danger was real. But I knew I wanted to find out.

There was no time to think. I was far too late for breakfast to do anything but run. I skidded into the refectory, the latest I had ever been. All round me the nuns stood like penguins. They had finished breakfast and were ready to file out. I waited in the doorway, wishing I had decided to go hungry.

Reverend Mother moved from her place in a stately procession of one. I hoped that she might pass me in a mystic trance, so I could sneak to my place unobserved. But she saw me and smiled down from her great height.

'How nice for you to spend a few days with Cathy Weston,' she said.

I felt paralysed, speechless as a rabbit. My mouth opened and shut like a natterjack toad. I could think of nothing to say. Reverend Mother is quite used to these conversations with awe-struck schoolgirls.

'I'm sure the sea air will do you good,' she continued, 'bring some colour into those cheeks.'

'Yes, I'm sure it will,' I said, then ran out of words again.

'Enjoy yourself, my child.'

'Thank you, Reverend Mother.'

She glided on her way, so pleased at having arranged the visit that I felt mean and nasty at not wanting to go. I poured myself a cup of tea from the urn and thought that four days could not last for ever. But they felt as though they could.

After breakfast I went upstairs to pack. As I said earlier, I have no clothes, so it did not take long. I shut the suitcase and made my bed. Then there was nothing to do but grind my teeth until Mrs Weston arrived.

Then I had an idea which I am really rather ashamed to write down, but I am not going to leave out anything that might help unravel the tangle and this was part of it.

I was thinking what a waste of time it was to stay with Mrs Weston, when Cathy did not want to see me and I did not want to go. I knew that the moment I returned to Belvedere, I would not want to fritter another second on Mrs Weston. I decided to write her a thank you letter and leave it ready to post when I returned. Like all great ideas, it was simple.

It was difficult to think what to say about my visit, especially when I had never even been there. I knew it was a town by the sea, so I said how pretty it was. I mentioned the sea air and how Reverend Mother had said it had brought some colour into my cheeks. That got me over the page. Many thanks for having me. Best wishes for the New Year and I was finished. I put it in an envelope, found Cathy's letter and copied out the address and stuck on a stamp. Then there was nothing to do again.

Across the passage from my bedroom door was a huge window, facing across the front of Belvedere. I flattened my nose against the glass and looked at the dark trees of the Wilderness.

'If I see him in daylight, then he is lying to me about being afraid to be seen,' I said, hoping that no one would come out from the trees. There was no one crossing the frosty fields either; but he might easily have gone during breakfast, or while I was packing.

Mrs Weston's car crunched across the gravel at last. I picked up my suitcase and gave one last look round my room, with its slithery Tudor roses. I adjusted my face until I looked like a polite and grateful child. It took some doing! Then I walked downstairs, leaving the thank you letter lying on the bedside table.

Ten

Who is Adam?

CATHY'S HOUSE was painted an angry crimson. It stood out among the faded houses along the sea front like a telephone kiosk at the North Pole. I guessed it was going to be her house before we stopped in front of it. The colour matched Mrs Weston.

We had not talked much during the drive from Belvedere. I was scared of Mrs Weston. I felt like a criminal when she turned her flashing spectacles on me and hoped I was never hauled in chains before her.

Cathy was out when we arrived and her brother Andrew mumbled when asked where she was. We drank some coffee. Andrew jogged round the kitchen in football shorts balancing the ball from his knee to his foot and back again. He was chewing some gum and the noise sounded like a pig walking through mud. He had large red ears and his wrists and knees were knobbly beyond the wildest nightmares of knobbliness. When he spoke of Cathy, his lip curled. I had always wanted an elder brother, but when I saw Andrew I realised the gods had been good to me after all.

Cathy had still not returned by the time I had unpacked. I sat on the spare bed in her room and stared out of the window. The visit was going to be even worse than I feared.

'Andrew, take Elizabeth outside and show her the beach!' called Mrs Weston in a bright and bossy voice. Andrew appeared in the bedroom doorway, a football under one arm.

'Have you got your bucket and spade?' he said sarcastically. There was nothing for it. Visitors have to be polite. I followed him downstairs, hating the back of his head.

The front door clanged and Andrew set off across the windswept road, dribbling his football expertly in front of him.

From the front doorstep, the little town was quite pretty. It was strung along the edge of a sandy bay, tall pink, yellow and grey houses. A spindly pier stalked out to sea on stiff black legs. The far end of it was twisted and crunched, like a broken toy. Seagulls perched carelessly on the crumpled railings.

'Why is the pier like that?' I called to Andrew, in an attempt at conversation.

'Storm.' He shouted over his shoulder and kicked his football against the post where the lifebelt hung.

I closed my eycs and tried to pretend I was somewhere else. A huge knot of homesickness swirled inside me and I was afraid I was going to cry in front of that dreadful Andrew. Time for a change! I was Napoleon on St Helena. A solitary, tragic figure staring stonily out to sea. Exiled for life. I set my jaw and slipped my hand inside my coat.

'Long live Emperor Napoleon!' 'Vive l'Empereur!'

The cries were fainter now, only a memory of vanished glory.

'Hullo Beth,' said a voice.

I opened my eyes and there was Cathy, her long hair blowing across her face. She flicked a glance across the road and added with the briefest of smiles,

'I see you've met Andrew.'

'Yes.'

I scowled at the view, not knowing what to say next. Blood was probably thicker than water and there was nothing I could truthfully say about Andrew that would be polite. I stealthily withdrew Napoleon's hand from inside his coat and hoped that Cathy had not seen him being exiled for life. But if she had, she might only have thought I was scratching.

'Did you get my letter?' asked Cathy, in an offhand manner.

'No, I didn't,' I said, when I should have said 'What letter?' My face gave me away and my cheeks began to burn.

Cathy's face buttoned up. The Art Mistress always says she looks like one of Botticelli's Three Graces. This time she looked like one of the Three Graces with toothache and it was all my fault.

'It doesn't matter anyway,' she added in a pale voice and crossed the road. She did not look back. I suddenly realised just how dreadful the next four days were going to be and wished I could crank a handle that would make them churn by faster. Andrew was awful, Mrs Weston terrifying and Cathy's feelings were hurt. I wondered what Mr Weston would be like and if I could run away. I could not have felt more isolated alone on the moon.

Mr Weston turned out to be surprisingly interesting. He looked like an Apostle, with a shining dome of a head and a bushy beard. I felt he should be dressed in flowing garments instead of trousers and a jersey. He was a scientist, which is not at all the sort of career one expects from an Apostle. But I liked him and admired the way he lived in the centre of a hurricane, allowing it to roar around him while he remained peaceful and unflustered.

When I say hurricane, I really mean it. Mrs Weston was so busy that the rest of us had to whirl about as though we were all on some giant roundabout and would be flung off if we relaxed.

The next morning was Saturday. Mrs Weston was wearing a white overall, boiling chestnuts, peeling sprouts, dictating notes for an article on child crime to a tape recorder lurking amongst the pots and pans and making mince pies on an industrial scale. From upstairs came the tortured cries of Andrew's violin, like someone treading on a cat. Cathy was bashing stamps on to a heap of Christmas cards on the draining board, making all the dishes jump. But Mr Weston sat alone and calm, absorbed in assembling a hot air balloon from a kit spread on the dresser.

'Alfred, I thought that toy was for your godson!'

'Must make sure it works,' said Mr Weston, with no trace of guilt. I lolled against the draining board, wishing I could help with the balloon.

'Beth dear, if you've nothing to do, give me a hand with these mince pies.'

'Certainly, Mrs Weston,' I said, remembering Sister Emmanuel's words about being polite and helpful. I rolled up my sleeves.

There were hundreds of mince pies for an ex-prisoners' Christmas dinner. I organised them into an assembly line ready for the oven, stacking the lids in a pile at one end.

'My, you are a good worker!' said Mrs Weston in tones of unconcealed surprise. 'I see I can leave that job to you while I do the sprouts.'

It was a massive order from overseas. The Tooty Frooty Pie Company's honour was at stake. The cutting machines clattered their way through miles of flattened pastry and the air was thick with flour as I dashed to and fro, passing down the line of pies clapping the lids on so fast that I might have been mistaken for a robot. Tray after tray was thrust into the oven by my nimble hands. Every shelf was packed. At last the final pie was in the oven. The midnight shift was over. I staggered wearily towards the works canteen...

'What a lot of mincemeat you seem to have left,' said Mrs Weston and the works canteen faded away.

'Mincemeat!' I said in a wobbly voice. 'Was I supposed to put mincemeat in them?'

'What *did* you put in them?' asked Mrs Weston, suddenly looking like the Counsel for the Prosecution.

'Nothing,' I said, feeling worse every minute. 'Only the lids.'

A shout of laughter from the other end of the kitchen.

'Hollow pies!' chuckled Mr Weston. 'Do-it-yourself pies! Put in your own fillings!'

'I have never heard of anything so incompetent in all my life!' snorted Mrs Weston as she salvaged a tray of hollow pies from the oven. 'A girl of your age...'

'I'm sorry,' I said lamely. I quite agreed with her. The pies looked dreadful. The lids had sunk and mere words could not undo the damage.

'Shall I make some more?' I offered.

'I think not, Elizabeth,' said Mrs Weston in a voice snippy like a pair of secateurs.

'Come on,' said Cathy, rescuing me. 'Let's go and post these Christmas cards.'

We walked along the seafront and turned up the main street. I felt ashamed and trembly. If I closed my eyes I could see rows of people all saying 'a girl of your age...' Oh when would I start being sensible? Would it happen suddenly?

'Have you done any Christmas shopping?' asked Cathy in an attempt at lightening our mood.

'No,' I said, 'but I want to get something for the nuns.'

I had not one single idea in my head. We jostled along the crowded street looking through the windows until I saw a bookshop.

'I must buy a book on the stars,' I said, and plunged inside.

'Stars!' said Cathy as I came out with a beginners' book in my hand. 'What do you want to know about them for?'

'Oh, it's interesting,' I said, remembering that Adam had made me promise not to tell anyone. Cathy shrugged her shoulders and struggled through the crowds into Woolworths.

'How many nuns are there in the Community?' I asked her when I drew up alongside.

'I've really no idea. I thought you were the one who knew all about the far side!'

'My, we are in a bate!' I said and passed down the hat counter trying on all the hats. I made a face to match each hat in the mirror and began to feel more cheerful. Cathy went by looking like a lemon. I could see she was jealous about the far side.

I wondered what to give the nuns for Christmas. They weren't interested in the tinselly side of it, bath salts and pink fluffy slippers. Anyway I did not have much money, not enough for a present for everyone. It would be dreadful to leave some of them out by mistake. If only there was something...

Then I saw a mound of daffodil bulbs. I knew that was the answer. Nuns love green and growing things. There were enough bulbs for every nun I knew and more besides, in case there were lots of very old and frail nuns that I had never even heard of. Even bedridden nuns could watch daffodils grow.

On the way out of Woolworths the crowd pressed me against the fishing tackle counter and on it lay a beautiful horn-handled dagger. It looked out of place, surrounded by bright plastic floats and gaily-coloured maggot pots. It looked like something from long ago. All at once I knew that I wanted to give it to Adam. It cost all the rest of my money.

'Who is that for?' asked Cathy as I lowered it reverently on top of the daffodil bulbs. I looked up startled. I had not expected her to be beside me.

'Just someone,' I said in a casual voice.

'Just someone!' Cathy imitated my voice as I walked ahead of her towards the doors.

'Just someone!'

I felt she was working up a head of steam and began to hum in a nonchalant manner. It made matters worse.

'You are altogether too mysterious, Elizabeth Lorimer!' she said, overtaking me by the door. 'First you buy a book on the stars and now you've splurged all your money on a knife for "just someone".'

She paused, hot and pink with rage. Suddenly her eyes widened.

'I know what it is!' she shrieked, with a wild laugh that silenced the whole shop. 'You bought it for Andrew!' and she collapsed across the peanut counter, shaking with laughter.

'I have not fallen in love,' I roared, hardly aware of the circle of startled shoppers. 'And if I did, I would never ever in a trillion years choose a twit like your brother! It is not for Andrew. I bought it for Adam.'

'Who is Adam?'

Cathy called after me as I stumped furiously down the main street, my cheeks ablaze.

I walked straight along the seafront, past the crimson house and on towards the pier. Cathy followed at a distance, mournfully like a stray dog.

'Who is Adam?' she called again and I began to think about it.

When I first saw Adam, I felt he was teasing

me for his own amusement. I had made a fool of myself (Anne Boleyn and all that jazz) and he had carried on the game. But even then, he seemed different from ordinary people. He seemed to be playing the same game as me, but I did not know for sure.

It was the second time that I had the first inklings that it was not just a game; that even if Adam had no hawk, the dangers he spoke of were real dangers. One thing was certain, even if everything else about him was make-believe, he really *was* afraid. It was the way that he said:

'What do you know of the man without a hawk?' as if it were really important, something to do with here and now.

'Only that Master Owen prepared a place for him,' I had replied (really as part of his game).

But I saw by his face, by his decision to trust me, that the danger was real and he had accepted me as a friend. He needed me.

'You share a name with our Sovereign Lady the Queen,' I remembered him saying and I suddenly realised with a thud that it was not our Queen Elizabeth he was talking about, but the one who lived four hundred years ago. In the days of Father Gerard.

I walked along the pier. Some of the floor-boards were missing and far below the sea swirled and sucked. I did not feel it was a danger. Adam's danger seemed more real. I held on to the cold black railings and faced out to sea.

'Adam is a ghost,' I told a watching seagull, trying out the words to see if they frightened me. But I knew I was not afraid. He might have lived before me, but he was a real ordinary person and he was also my friend. I wanted to help him. I felt happy, swamped in happiness, enough to overflow the whole world, and tremendously full of excitement.

I saw Cathy, standing alone and worried by the desolate amusement arcade.

'The pier's not safe,' she called.

'OK Cathy, I'm coming back!'

How mean I was. I felt sorry. I knew I had been beastly to Cathy for a long time, for such a mixture of reasons. It wasn't her fault she had a home and I did not. I hoped she understood. Perhaps I could tell her some day.

But I could not tell her about Adam. I walked back along the pier and said he was someone I'd met in the summer holidays. But inside me I hugged the secret that I had met him a few days ago and would see him again on Christmas Eve. In the meantime, I had to learn about the stars.

Eleven

The Little Bear

THERE IS NO PLACE more desolate on God's earth than a seaside town on a wet Sunday afternoon.

The sea was flat and stippled with rain drops. A sodden cloud smothered the pier, pressing it into the water.

'Do you think the weather will clear up?' I said to no-one in particular and my breath made a fog on the window pane.

'I hope so,' said Mr Weston, peering out of the window. 'My balloon is ready to go up.'

'Your balloon indeed!'

Mrs Weston flashed a look at him through her metallic spectacles.

'I shall have to post it tomorrow,' he said, 'there are only three days left till Christmas.'

'If it doesn't clear,' I said, thinking aloud, 'I won't be able to see the stars.'

'I can't think why you're so keen on stars all of a sudden,' said Cathy from her place on the hearth rug. 'You never even noticed them before.'

'It's a hobby,' I said, trying to think of some satisfactory explanation. 'Sister Columba said I ought to have a hobby and so I've chosen the stars.'

A disbelieving silence greeted this. I opened

my book and studied the map of the night sky, hoping I had laid a false trail.

'Look at the stars and find the Little Bear. That is all I shall tell you now, for your own sake.'

Adam's words rang so clearly in my head that I looked round the room afraid I might have spoken aloud.

Stars and danger. What possible link could they have with one another? How could the stars be a secret?

Only one thing was clear. Adam was afraid for someone whose life might be in danger. He had come to Belvedere to find someone he could trust and that person was me. Adam trusted me and I would not let him down. I began to think about this person whose life Adam had said would be at risk if he could not find someone to trust. It could not be Tom. When I asked 'Who is Tom?' Adam had replied 'He *was* my brother.'

I suddenly saw Adam's face; the way his eyes had flashed that first night when he said 'It is hard to accept the death of those whom we love.'

He knew what he was talking about all right. He knew what it was like to wake up morning after morning feeling it had all been a bad dream and then realising it was true. Adam knew, and he had learned to live with it. That took some doing.

'Cathy dear, why don't you find something useful to do?'

Mrs Weston's steel knitting needles clicked to and fro.

'I wish you had a hobby, like Beth's astronomy or Andrew's football.'

Cathy sat up and stretched.

'Beth is not interested in stars. She just daydreams all the time. You should hear Sister Columba talking about Beth's castles in the air.'

'I'm sure that's not true,' commented Mrs Weston, but she did not sound convinced. Not that I blamed her, not after the Great Mince Pie Disaster.

I began to think about my castles in the air. Was it true? Did I really daydream all the time? Even Adam had teased me about it, calling me Mistress Boleyn. Oh well, that was just the way I was made. Crocodiles had teeth and I had day-dreams.

But now I had something else as well. Sunset on Christmas Eve. Then I would find out what it was all about. But how was I going to make the days go by? Three whole days.

I jumped out of my chair and paced up and down the sitting room, trying to squash the excitement that was fizzing inside me. Mrs Weston's knitting sprang off her lap and followed me round the back of her armchair. She retrieved it in silence.

'Oh I am sorry,' I said, trying to unravel my feet.

'Come on,' said Cathy, hauling herself off the hearthrug. 'I've thought of a hobby. Making fudge.'

There is a lot to be said for making fudge. It helps to pass the time. We dropped spoonfuls into a bowl of cold water to see if it was ready to set. By the time it was cooked, we seemed to have tasted half the fudge. Cathy and I lolled against the stove when we had finished, waiting for the remains to set. There was a sticky and comfortable silence while we licked the wooden spoons.

'Do you want to go back to school for Christmas?' said Cathy.

'I do in a way,' I said, trying not to show just how much I wanted to. 'I want to see Reverend Mother playing with a balloon at a Christmas party. Besides, I've promised to sing for Mother Christina.'

'Poor Mother Christina—what torture for her!'

Cathy shut her eyes and shuddered.

'Better than if you sang,' I retorted. 'At least it will be in tune.'

'Well you can come back here again afterwards, if you like,' said Cathy.

'Thanks,' I said, 'if Dad can't come back, it might be nice...'

But I left the sentence unfinished. It was impossible to imagine anything beyond Christmas Eve, when I would see Adam again.

'My lucky day!' said Mr Weston coming into the kitchen and circling the fudge like a hungry shark. 'The rain has stopped, so now I can see if that balloon really works.'

The balloon did work. The little fire in its basket burned so well that the balloon soared in the air with the black thread that Mr Weston had hoped to tether it by trailing along behind it at rooftop level.

'The fuel will soon be finished,' said Mr Weston confidently as we trotted after it along the marine parade.

But the balloon turned sharp left on a breeze that had sprung up out of nowhere and zoomed out to sea. Mr Weston stood on the beach, unable to believe its treachery. It soared and dwindled until it was a red dot in the sky.

'Poor Daddy. He has lost his toy!' said Cathy, smirking at me.

'My toy! What nonsense,' said Mr Weston. 'I was only testing it. At least I know it works,' he added mournfully.

'Perhaps it will arrive in France or Belgium just in time to make a Christmas present for someone,' I said, to comfort him. He laughed.

'You are more fortunate, Beth. Stars don't float away like that. Look, the evening star is just coming out and the night is clearing up.'

It was true. The clouds were clearing away. With any luck I would be able to look for the Little Bear when it was dark.

Later that evening I stood on the promenade with my book and a torch. The street lamps made the sky a dull orange as ragged clouds reflected their light. I walked a little way out along the pier. It was darker there.

'The Stars in Winter' was the name of my map and one edge was called 'the northern horizon'. Which way up was I supposed to hold it and where on earth was North? I twisted round and held the map above me like a hat, trying to match it to the sky. No good. Perhaps it was the wrong way up. I put the map on the boards and consulted that way, peering at the stars from between my legs as though I was going to do a somersault. I was sure the Astronomer Royal never adopted such an undignified posture for star gazing. Something was wrong with my technique.

'You are a crackpot!' I heard Cathy's voice as she came along the pier towards me. 'What are you trying to do?'

'Can you see the Little Bear?' I asked (after all that could not be giving any secrets away).

'I can see the little donkey,' said Cathy.

But she helped me after that. She knew which way was North, so I found the Little Bear. It suddenly sprang out of the sky and I could not understand how I had not seen the pattern before. Seven stars clustered together. The pole star was very bright, but it looked rather ordinary. I wondered what the secret was.

'All the other stars seem to rotate round the pole star,' I read aloud, 'but do not in fact do so.'

'How fascinating,' said Cathy. 'Come on, let's go back before Andrew eats all the fudge.'

I saw the Little Bear from the bedroom window that night, after Cathy had gone to sleep. I lay watching it for ages, spinning a dream of saving a priest from the Queen's men, on a starry night long ago. Adam was there and he dropped on one knee and thanked me.

'It was nothing,' I murmured. Then I was suddenly hit by a terrible thought.

'If Adam is a ghost,' I said, sitting bolt upright in bed, 'if he is a ghost, then I can do nothing to help him. The danger he was talking about happened four hundred years ago. It is all over and, what is worse, it must have gone wrong or he would not still be haunting the pavilion, trying to find some help. Ghosts only haunt when they cannot rest in peace!'

I looked across at the dark hump of Cathy in the next bed.

'Cathy,' I whispered urgently. 'I want to talk about a ghost!'

No answer. I was glad in a way. I knew that I had promised not to tell anyone. Even if it made no difference, I had to try and keep my word until after Christmas Eve.

Twelve

The Thank-You Letter

WHEN I AM an old lady, nodding by the fire, I shall still wake up with a start every time I remember breakfast on Christmas Eve.

It started peacefully enough. I had made an island of my porridge, and was about to cause a tidal wave that would shatter the tranquil lives of the islanders, when Mr Weston came in with the morning mail, and plopped it on the table.

I glanced up, hoping perhaps for a letter from Dad, and on top of the pile I saw an envelope addressed to Mrs Weston, in my own handwriting! In a flash I realised that someone had tidied my bedroom, and posted the letter on the bedside table. It lay there, dominating the whole room. I longed to cry 'Fire!' or fall down in a dead faint to create a diversion, but I was frozen to my chair with horror. Mrs Weston still had not seen it. She sat behind her paper crunching toast.

At last I thought of a plan. I would pretend to reach for the marmalade, and scoop up the letter on the way. My hand moved, hovered towards the letter, and at precisely the same moment Mrs Weston lowered her newspaper and attacked her morning mail. She picked up the envelope and slit it open.

The world swayed. I felt as though I was falling—falling down a colossal precipice, weightless and panic stricken. I watched Mrs Weston read the letter, a puzzled frown on her face. She finished it, handed it in silence to her husband, and turned to look at me. For the first time, I understood the emotions of a rabbit helpless before the gaze of a boa constrictor. In fact, I felt that being swallowed alive would be preferable to meeting her gaze.

'It was... you see...' The rabbit blundered on, heedless of its words. 'You see I did not want to come and stay,' I heard my voice say, 'so I pretended I had already been and wrote the letter, then I would not have to waste time on it when I got back...' My voice trailed away. I did not have to be a mind reader to realise I was only making things worse. Mrs Weston looked at me as though my criminal record stretched back to the dawn of time.

'Well, Elizabeth!' she said at last, in a voice that made even the teacups tremble. 'I do not know what *you* learn at school, but it is certainly not good manners! In all my life, I have never met a child who lived so completely in a daydream. First the mince pie fiasco, and now this!'

'I'm very sorry,' I said, and my voice seemed to belong to someone else.

'Take my advice, young lady,' she continued. 'Sooner or later you will have to come down to earth. You can't spend the rest of your life in the clouds.'

'Don't be too hard on the child,' said Mr Weston gently. 'It is a very nice letter. She just got her time sequence muddled up, that's all.'

While I was packing, Cathy came into the bedroom. I looked out of the window to hide the tears that kept trickling down my cheeks. I blinked fiercely but they kept on coming.

I remembered hearing someone say 'Stop the World! I want to get off!' It seemed like a good idea.

'Cheer up, Beth,' said Cathy. 'It will all seem funny one day.'

It was kind of her to say so, but I did not think it would, not for a thousand years.

There was only one thing about that breakfast that I ever want to remember. It was Mr Weston saying 'She just got her time sequence muddled up, that's all.'

'Do you think time can get muddled up?' I asked him cautiously as he drove me back towards Belvedere. He was a scientist, so I thought he would know about that sort of thing.

'I don't see why not,' he said. 'There is nothing in the laws of physics which forbids the transfer of information from the future to the past.'

'Information—what do you mean?'

'Like in telepathy. It is called precognition when someone knows and describes something that has not yet happened, even down to the last detail, and it does happen. There are plenty of well documented examples of it.'

'Do you think there could be action from the future to the past as well?' I asked, afraid that I sounded halfwitted.

'There is nothing against it,' he said cheerfully. 'Scientists' ideas about the relationship of space and time are changing daily. We are no longer as certain as our forefathers were that time is an ever-rolling stream. We are only just beginning to find out about it.'

'I am glad!' I said with such relief that Mr Weston looked at me quizzically.

'I don't think you can explain away that letter by saying that time went backwards,' he chuckled. 'You'll have to put that one down to experience.'

'I will,' I told him, 'and I'm very sorry, because I really *did* enjoy staying with you.'

* * *

Lunch was eaten in silence as the nuns were still in retreat. Lots of them smiled at me but no one spoke. I sat at the end of one of the long polished tables, alone with my thoughts.

One really good thing had come from my visit to the Westons. I knew from Mr Weston that the future and the past could get mixed up. So I would be able to help Adam after all.

On the way out of lunch, the Mistress of the Novices touched me on the shoulder.

'Would you like to help Sister Cecily bring down the figures for the crib?' she said softly.

I nodded. The silence was catching.

I followed Sister Cecily up the stairs, past the door of my room and on down to the wing where the nuns slept. Sister Cecily turned and said,

'The figures are stored here, in an empty cell.'

I tried to look calm and everyday and I followed Sister Cecily down the passage, past rows of identical doors. I almost expected peepholes in them—like prison cells in films.

I was going to store up every tiny detail, to be

able to tell it all to Cathy next term. The bleakness, the pallet on the floor, with one horsehair blanket. The pitcher of cold water standing in an enamel bowl for morning ablutions. Perhaps they did not even have a bed at all, but just slept on the bare boards like the desert Fathers (except that they slept on rock).

Sister Cecily opened a door and I followed her in—agog.

The cell was small and whitewashed. There was an ordinary basin with hot and cold taps. A table and chair and a black iron bed. It really looked quite homely.

Trying to squash my disappointment, I furtively prodded the bed as Sister Cecily unpacked the statuettes from a large packing case.

The bed looked like my school bed and felt like it, down to the last lump. No nails—no boards. I sat on it. Deflated and depressed. Another balloon had gone bang.

Then for the first time I felt a small curl of panic inside me. Instead of fussing about whether or not I could help Adam, I started to wonder whether or not he was real. What if Mrs Weston was right and I did live in a world of make-believe? Perhaps I was mad. A split personality. Half of me being Beth Lorimer and half being totally insane.

'Wake up, Beth!' said Sister Cecily, her arms full of plaster shepherds. 'You carry Melchior. Mind his crown doesn't fall off.'

I tucked the swarthy king under my arm and trudged after her down the passage. Did people *know* if they were mad, I wondered. Or was part of the madness not knowing?

Thirteen

Wilderness at Sunset

THE PAVILION AT SUNSET looked as though it had been neglected for hundreds of years (which it had). I pulled the velvet cloak round me and shivered. I was scared and miserable. I was scared of the Wilderness at dusk but most of all I was scared that Adam would not be there. What if I had imagined the whole thing from start to finish?

Time passed. The shadows deepened. Whatever happened, I was going to have to walk back through the Wilderness in the dark. I sat there, not caring. There was no supper that night as the nuns were fasting, so there was nothing to be late for. But I did not want to go back to Belvedere. I did not want to meet Sister Emmanuel, who had said she would cook me beans on toast in the Infirmary kitchen. She would know something was wrong and she would want to help. But no one could, outside my dreams or madness.

I pulled the sheath knife from under my cloak and turned it over in my hand. I had so often rehearsed giving it to Adam. I decided to throw it away in the fishpond, so that it never reminded me of him again.

The Angelus bell rang from far away, a sad

insistent tong, tong. I stood in the doorway and looked up at the sky. The moon was rising and I was a lunatic. I wanted to howl like a wolf.

The stars were pinpoints of brightness crystal clear. I saw the Little Bear. Surely some of it had happened? I remembered Adam asking me to sing the Te Deum. Why should I imagine something like that? It was not even interesting, being asked to sing a stodgy old Latin hymn.

Singing! The idea flooded into me so that I swayed against the threshold. All at once the bits of the puzzle fell into place and I could not understand how I had been so thick.

Both times I had met Adam, I had been singing at the top of my voice. The first time when I was Anne Boleyn and then the next morning when I was thinking about Good King Wenceslas and his royal picnic. Perhaps singing made the difference, woke the echoes of long ago and made him be there in some way—part of the echoes.

It was hard to sing with my throat dry and lumpy in case it did not work. But it was my last chance. I took a deep breath and sang:

'Alas, my love, you do me wrong
To treat me so discourteously,
For I have loved you so long
Delighting in your company.'

It was true. I realised that as I sang. Adam was special. My voice trailed away in despair. I swallowed and continued:

'Greensleeves was all my joy
And oh Greensleeves was my delight,'

Then the song soared high, way up beyond my reach into the black sky:

> 'Greensleeves was my heart of gold
> And who but my lady Greensleeves.'

I let him finish. I was too happy to speak, let along sing. A shadow moved out from the pavilion.

'You came at last,' he said, 'I have waited so long.'

'I was afraid I would never see you again. But I looked at the stars and I was certain you had told me to find the Little Bear.'

'Show it to me,' said Adam, standing on the doorstep beside me.

'There it is, above the branches of that witchlike old tree.'

'And which is the brightest star in the Little Bear?' he asked in a businesslike voice. I felt as though I was taking an exam.

'The pole star,' I said. 'At his tail.'

Adam nodded. He did not look at me but turned his face up to the sky. In the moonlight he looked fierce and triumphant.

'Tonight I will ask you to move the pole star.'

'What do you mean?' I said cautiously.

Perhaps he was the one who was mad. I had expected him to be a bit more romantic and grateful than this, after I had braved the Wilderness at twilight for his sake.

'There is a closet in Belvedere, high in the far wing,' he continued. 'The room is small and its walls are covered with Tudor roses...'

'I know that room...' I burst in but Adam cut me short.

'I have not much time. You must listen to what I say.'

'Tell me then.'

'In this room Master Owen made a cunning device that opens a secret door. It was Sir Jocelyn's late wife, the Lady Alice, who had him make it last year. God rest her soul.'

(I had heard of Sir Jocelyn, a fat timeserver whose family had grown rich through the pickings from the monasteries. It was amazing to learn that his wife had been a Catholic. I was sure he had not known a thing about it.)

'There is no one at Belvedere now who knows the secret of the rose room,' Adam continued, 'although some of the household will make their way to the room at midnight, hoping to hear Mass this Christmastide, beyond the secret door.'

'But how can I help them?'

'Last winter my brother Tom, newly ordained and come from France, was invited to Belvedere as a family friend for the Christmas feast. He went because this was what he was taught to do at the priests' college.

'Go first to a great house and then see if you can bring the comforts of the religion to any who have remained loyal to it. A word dropped here and there in the kitchens or stables will usually bring good simple folk, still true in their hearts to the old faith.'

That would have been the way, I thought. Country folk would not have changed their beliefs because they wanted high position or great wealth. They would have remained faithful.

'But it was Midnight last Christmas Eve,' Adam continued, 'when Sir Jocelyn had fallen asleep at the high table, that the Lady Alice rose from her place in the Great Hall and, taking a candle from a sconce, signed for Tom to follow her. She led him up to the rose room.'

I knew the way they went, out from the chapel, along the passage and up the twisting stairs towards my room. I could almost see it happening. The great lady and the ardent young priest.

'She showed him how seven of the Tudor roses are so set that they make up the constellation of the Little Bear. She twisted the pole star to the right and a hidden catch was released.'

'And then the fireplace?' I guessed.

Adam shook his head. 'Not the fireplace. Master Owen does not use the same tricks twice! It is the seventh floorboard from the door, Tom told me. Once the pole star has been twisted round, the floorboard is free to swing over. There are steps that pass under the wall and up into a hidden chapel in the rooftops.'

'The pole star and the seventh floorboard,' I said. 'I can do that, at midnight. But where is the priest?'

'Tonight, if the muddy roads have not held them up, a stage wagon will come, bringing the mummers and jesters with all their hobby horses, monsters, pipes, bells and drums, for the feasting tomorrow. There is one jester who will wear the head of a hawk and be among the merriest of the troupe. This night you must guide the hawk to the rose room. He will expect someone to approach him and say "Follow me".'

'Follow me,' I repeated. That sounded easy enough!

'At midnight in the rose room, the people of Belvedere will come, those who are still of the old faith. You must open the door and lead them to the hidden chapel, closing the entrance behind you. There is an escape across the rooftops if anything should go wrong.'

He paused and looked at me.

'Do you understand?'

I nodded. 'But how will I know who to trust?'

'Philippa knows, Lady Alice's maid. But she does not know the secret of the rose room. In the chapel is a chest that serves for a table and in that chest there is all that is necessary to change a hawk into a priest.'

To think there really was a chapel right next to my room! I could hardly wait to get back and start discovering it all.

'Now for the vital part,' Adam said, 'and the reason why I am here. I have a message for the hawk that was passed to me last week. If you fail to give it to him, his life may well be lost. He intends to leave after midnight mass and ride through the night to another household. You must say to him: "Do not go to Crepping, there is a plot to take you there." '

I repeated the words, still hardly able to believe it was all happening.

'Now tell me all you have to do,' Adam said and I told him, then I added.

'But Adam, there is one thing I do not understand.'

'And what is that?'

'If your brother told you about the seven roses before he... before...'

'Before he was martyred,' said Adam grimly. 'Go on.'

'Then why can't you come to Belvedere tonight and warn the hawk yourself?'

'Because if I am not at home within the hour, my father will guess what I am doing and like as not tell Sir Jocelyn.'

'Your own father—betray you!'

The words were out before I realised. I wished I had never said them. Adam was silent for a while and when he spoke again his voice was bitter.

'My father says that to lose one son is to sacrifice enough. He wants me to have nothing more to do with "Romish priests". But I cannot do what he asks! I gave my word to Tom when I saw him in prison. Tom was not afraid. He gave me his missal and his silver cross and chain as merrily as though they were tokens at Christmas-tide. Do you know what he told me? He said "Fear itself has taken away all fear", and asked me not to mourn him.'

Adam looked round and added 'But I *have* been afraid, hiding in these woods like an outlaw, fearful of being seen so far from home.'

'But why are you coming to the feast tomorrow, if Catholics are forbidden to travel far from their homes?'

A sigh seemed to be drawn right up from Adam's boots, then he said all in a rush,

'My father is to tell Sir Jocelyn that he will take the Oath of Allegiance at the next sessions and then Sir Jocelyn will welcome him to tomorrow's feast and renew our leasehold on his land.'

I did not know what to say. I knew what it

meant. Adam's father was turning his back on all that he believed to be true.

'I can only see it as a question of right and wrong,' Adam continued, in the voice of one who has gone over it all a thousand times before, 'but my father says there are other matters he must consider. We are Sir Jocelyn's tenants and were nearly turned out of house and home after Tom was captured. My father has been heavily fined, both in goods and chattels. Then there is my mother's health. She has been sick in mind and melancholy since Tom died. But Tom trusted me. He had courage and I cannot betray his trust.'

'I think that Tom would be proud of his brother,' I said gently. 'You are the bravest person I know.'

Then I remembered my present for him and held it out.

'Look, this is to wish you a merry Christmas and if I could do anything to make your Christmas happier, believe me, I would.'

Adam took the dagger and slid it out of its sheath. The blade flashed in the moonlight.

'Why, it is beautiful,' he said admiringly, 'and polished so fine.'

Then he looked at me and shook his head sadly.

'I have nothing for you, Beth. I had no thoughts for Christmas tokens, only the message I must pass to the hawk.'

'I don't want anything...' I began, but he cut me short.

'I know what I shall give you and you must not refuse it.'

He pulled the silver chain from out of his jerkin and fastened it round my neck.

I looked down at the cross as it shone against the folds of the grey velvet cloak.

'But Adam,' I said, ashamed that I had forced him into giving me a present, 'it is far too precious. I know what it means to you.'

'A life is precious,' Adam replied, 'and Tom would have wanted it so.'

Then he bent over my hand, brushed it with his lips and was gone.

I stood looking after him into the dark tree trunks. I heard horse's hooves striking on the frosty ground, thudding into the distance. Then I turned and floated back to Belvedere, my head full of all the things I had promised to do before midnight.

Fourteen

Let Midnight Never Come

I HAVE READ all that I have written so far and I don't want to go on. Up to now it all worked. Things did turn out OK. Adam was real and I did help him. I would like to write the end like that, but it was not the way it happened and it would not help me sort out the tangle. Stick to plain facts, I've told myself (using Mrs Weston's voice) and that is what I shall do.

Plain facts then. I floated back to Belvedere in a cloud of mystery and excitement. I was wondering where the stage wagon was, if it would manage on the roads. Good thing it is a frosty night, I remembered thinking, so its wheels won't get bogged down. I did not even begin to understand that the roads were covered with tarmac and the time was the twentieth century.

The nuns were in Chapel and the house was dark and silent. On my way down the Chapel passage I opened the door and stood on the threshold and looked in. A red light burned in front of the altar. I looked at the high windows, the vaulted ceiling and then turned towards the choir, where the nuns now knelt in silence above me. It must have been the minstrels' gallery, long ago. And the high table would have been on the dais at the far end of the room, where the altar now stood.

I walked slowly up to my room, enveloped in the past, treading the steps I knew that Tom and the Lady Alice had trodden on a Christmas Eve long ago. When I reached my room I looked at it with new eyes, as though it was the first time I had ever been there.

The roses were scattered at random on the walls, but it was easy once I knew their secret. I soon picked out the seven roses that made the Little Bear. I dragged my bed out of the way. It was crouching on top of the seventh floorboard.

I hesitated, afraid for the first time of the past that would come flooding back when I turned it. Adam would not be there, no one I knew. At least I knew my way round the house. The mummers would probably be in the Chapel, the great hall, and the hawk would be alert, waiting for someone to contact him.

I took a deep breath. It seemed unbelievable that I was about to meet one of the most exciting of all the priests who cheerfully risked death to bring the sacraments to those who remained loyal to the Catholic faith. I had not asked Adam who the hawk was. I already knew. I remembered what Father Lewis had said about him. 'He was so merry and full of tricks that not even his closest friends knew he was a man of God.' I was about to meet Father John Gerard and not only to meet him, but to pass on a message that would help to save his life.

I held my breath as I reached up to turn the pole star.

It would not budge. Why had I ever thought it would? I stood and looked at it. The sharp outlines of the Tudor rose petals were blurred by four centuries of paint. It was no longer a rose. It was a shapeless blob.

I grew desperate. I fought with the blob until my wrists ached and sweat poured on to my palms. My hands kept slipping and my knuckles bashed themselves against the solid wall. I leaned my head against the plaster and tried to think clearly. A knife. I had to scrape off the paint. Then the rose would move. I pulled off my cloak, flung it on the bed and ran to the Infirmary kitchen.

Sister Emmanuel was there, peacefully watching a saucepan of baked beans.

'Just in time,' she said with a gentle smile. 'I was beginning to think you had vanished into thin air.'

For once I was glad that everyone was in retreat and I did not have to talk as I ate the beans on toast. They tasted like wood and my hands trembled as I sliced the toast. I had to get back and work with that knife. I looked at my watch. Four and a half hours until midnight and perhaps the floorboard would be stuck in the same way.

I finished the beans and gulped down a glass of milk. Sister Emmanuel watched in tranquil silence.

'Thanks very much,' I said, running my plate and fork under the cold tap. I slipped the knife up my sleeve.

'I'll call for you just before midnight,' said Sister Emmanuel. 'It is a beautiful service. We sing the Office before it.'

'Thanks very much,' I said again and left the kitchen at the double.

Under the blue paint was white, further back green, that might even have seen Oliver Cromwell, then several layers of brown and cream, a yellow and finally what must have been the earliest layer of all, a rich royal red. The flakes of paint floated on to the floor as I chiselled away. At last the base of the rose was red all round and I was ready to move it again. But although I tried and tried until my hands were blistered, it did not budge by a hair's breadth. Perhaps the floorboard was jammed. I slid the knife up and down the cracks and against the skirting board. Still no good.

I began to realise that there was only one way to do it; that was to go back to Adam's time. Then I remembered singing. I sat up and sang, hoping no one would come in and see me hot and desperate, singing in front of a battered rose sticking out on the smooth blue wall.

Although I sang the whole of Greensleeves, nothing happened. So singing only worked when Adam was there too, wanting to get in touch with me. We made two sides of a bridge across the centuries. I was beaten and I flung myself down on the bed.

The next thing I knew, there was a tap on the door. Sister Emmanuel stood in the doorway, her prayer book in her hand. She looked very concerned to see me, hot, crumpled and still in my clothes in the middle of the night.

'Beth dear, are you all right?'

'Yes, it's nothing,' I mumbled, trying to remember where I was and what was happening. 'I fell asleep.'

'I'm just on the way to Chapel,' she said. 'Come if you want to. It is half past eleven.'

'Thanks, I'll come in a minute.'

She glided away, her veil floating out behind her.

When I reached the Chapel, quite a few people were there from the surrounding countryside. They all looked cheerful and modern. I wondered what had happened to the mummers and if the hawk was still waiting for someone to guide him to the rose room.

'Swing back the doors, captains of the guards,
Swing back, immemorial gates,
to let the King enter in triumph.'

The pure voices of the nuns rose and fell as they sang the psalms in the shadowy Choir. I knelt below them, in the pews, my face buried in my hands.

'Swing back the doors...' I repeated, as sadness swamped me like a tidal wave.

I had been so sure everything would work! But as I knelt there I realised that it was not just the priest's hole I had failed to find. If I could not change the time, then I could not warn the hawk. A priest was going to be betrayed into the hands of the Queen's men, condemned to an unspeakable death, all because of me.

If I had been honest, even at the last moment I could have let Adam know I did not belong to his time. But no! I had nodded away as he spoke of Sir Jocelyn, just as if the man was my guardian. All that I had done, all I had said had made Adam believe he could trust me, that I could do what he asked me to do at midnight. It did not matter to me who was Catholic or who was Protestant, those days were long over. It mattered that a man was going to die and it was my fault.

'Oh God,' I prayed, 'Let midnight never come!' But it did.

Fifteen

Black Christmas

BEFORE I WAS even awake, I was talking aloud. 'The hawk. What has happened to the hawk?'

I stared at the ceiling. Sadness pressed on my chest, hard as a paving slab. What had he done at midnight when no one came to him? Had he ridden on to Crepping, straight into the trap? Perhaps he had waited at Belvedere, knowing something had gone wrong, hiding among the mummers, wondering what to do next. Wondering and fearing. If he had waited, I might somehow be able to tell Adam. Adam might be able to warn him. I thought of getting out of bed and running up to the pavilion.

But it was no use. I knew Adam would not be there. I remembered his face in the moonlight the night before, triumphant. He had done his part. He had entrusted the message to me. I was the next link in the chain. The link that broke...

I rolled over, trying to blot out everything with a pillow. Gloating bullies would be questioning Father Gerard by now, before he was sent in chains to London to be tortured, to make him tell the names of all his contacts, perhaps even Adam.

Was it all pain and humiliation, the capture? Or did it feel remote, as though it was happening to someone else? He must have prepared for it in his mind, at least a thousand times. Did that make it any easier when the time came?

There was something crouching at the end of my bed. I sat up and stared at it. Long, black and bulgy, with a red ribbon like a festive sausage dog. Then I remembered. Christmas day! Whatever I did, I could not stop it. Christmas was rolling relentlessly onwards. The blackest Christmas of my life.

I flopped back, ignoring the stocking. Irrelevant. The Tudor rose was chipped and battered in the centre of the smooth blue wall, as though some maniac had singled it out for destruction. I was that maniac. It was going to need some explaining, but that did not matter. The only thing that mattered was that I had betrayed a priest into the hands of the priest hunters and there was nothing in this world that I could do to save him.

A tap on the door. Sister Emmanuel popped her head round, wreathed in Christmas smiles. Her face fell when she saw the stocking, still untouched at the end of my bed.

I woke up and saw it for the first time. It was not a very good bit of acting, and I knew she was not taken in. She sat on the bed and I reached out for the stocking and tried to show some enthusiasm, but I felt much nearer to howling like a lost dog.

'We should not have let you stay up for midnight Mass,' she said. 'You are overtired.'

'It's not that...' I began, but did not know how to continue. Sister Emmanuel nodded. I knew that she thought I was missing last

Christmas and it made me feel worse than ever. I did not deserve her sympathy.

We unpacked the stocking together. Lots of tiny presents, immaculately wrapped. I recognised some of the handwriting on them from my school reports. Every one was so kind. It was worse like that. I let the stocking drop limply on to the eiderdown.

'Come on, Beth, wash your face in cold water and you'll soon feel right as rain.'

Action. I stumped out of bed and crossed over to the basin. I caught sight of my reflection in the glass. Pink eyes in an anxious white face stared back at me. I turned on the cold tap.

'Mother Christina's bed is going to be wheeled into the choir for High Mass this morning,' Sister Emmanuel said. 'There is never room in the term time. She is so happy about it and is longing to hear you sing.'

'I'm not exactly feeling like a nightingale,' I began, rubbing a flannel over my face.

'You'll be much better if you can make someone else happy instead of sitting here brooding,' she said.

It was true. But my throat felt tight and hard, quite unable to sing.

'I've nothing to wear. She won't want to see me in my scruffy old jeans ...'

'What's wrong with this?'

Sister Emmanuel opened the cupboard and pulled out my Anne Boleyn dress, beautifully ironed. She looked as pleased as a conjuror at having remembered I wanted to wear it for Christmas.

'Oh yes,' I said, staring at it. The dress made

long ago seem impossibly far away, like the pageant. All futile make-believe. Why had I ever thought it would work? Why had I ever thought it was real?

After breakfast we all trooped out into the thin winter sunshine for a photograph. The nuns clustered like penguins, round elderly relations with concertinaed stockings. Sister Columba fought with her antique camera to record Christmas.

Adam would have a record of Christmas too, I thought. The day that his father ceased to be a man he could respect. The day his father renewed his lease with Sir Jocelyn and agreed to take the Oath of Allegiance at the next quarter sessions. The day of compromise.

There would be something else for him to remember too, when the news filtered back down the line to him. The day the chain broke, the weak link snapped and a priest was betrayed. Although I now knew there was nothing I could do to change it, I hoped that Adam would never believe that I had deliberately let the hawk ride into the trap. If only I could reach him!

I looked across the playing fields towards the wilderness, but I knew it was useless. There would be no two sides of the bridge across the centuries this time. On Christmas Day long ago, Adam would be riding with his father and mother to Belvedere for the midday feast. Even if there was a hawk among the mummers, Adam would never think it was Father Gerard, just another of the actors. There was no way...

I don't remember much about High Mass. I can't say I have ever paid less attention to what went on around me. The congregation snuffled and coughed, babies cried, nuns sang, incense rose in clouds and I knelt with my head in my hands wishing I could crawl into a hole and hide. I never even thought how peculiar I must look in my Anne Boleyn gear. I did not care a rap for what the twentieth century thought about anything.

'Beth, come up to the choir.'

Sister Cecily stood there. Mass was over, the congregation had melted away and the altar boy was snuffing the candles.

I held my skirts and climbed the spiral staircase from the Chapel to the choir. It was the minstrel's gallery once, but now it has rows of choir stalls, like semi-detached thrones, all down the walls. They are shiny with constant use because this is where the nuns spend half their lives, singing the Divine Office.

In the centre of the choir, just beside the lectern, was a high steel bed with black rubber wheels. It looked thoroughly out of place. I walked towards it, trying to be cheerful and full of Christmas spirit. Propped up on a wedge of pillows was a very old lady with calm blue eyes.

'This is Beth, Mother.'

Reverend Mother's voice was low and gentle. I stood by the bed and Mother Christina reached out a hand, translucent as bone china.

'Beth, my dear, will you sing a carol for us?'

I held her hand. Dry and frail. She was nearly a hundred. The oldest person I had ever seen. She had entered the convent when skirts were long and Queen Victoria sat on the throne. Just looking at her made me realise again the impossibility of going back through time, of the centuries that yawned between Adam and me. It was all over. I had to try and forget about it.

'What would you like me to sing?'

Mother Christina looked beyond me, over the balustrade, down into the Chapel. She looked at the crib beside the altar and smiled.

'Please will you sing "What Child is This". It is such a beautiful carol.'

It was the tune of Greensleeves. Why did I have to be reminded of it?

Sister Ambrose went to the organ and rattled briskly through the opening bars. I moved slightly away from the bed, nearer to the balustrade, took a deep breath and began:

> 'What child is this who laid to rest
> On Mary's lap is sleeping,
> Whom Angels greet with anthems sweet
> While shepherds watch are keeping . . .'

As I sang, I shut my eyes, trying to blot out the scene that flashed again and again, like a horrifying newsreel. Cobbled streets, jeering crowds, a man dragged on a hurdle, his face detached and peaceful, his soul in God only knew what torment.

> 'This, this is Christ the King
> Whom Shepherds watch and Angels sing . . .'

I thought of Adam and all that I had promised to do.

The candles were snuffed now, all but one. Its flame blurred and quavered in front of my eyes. I blinked fiercely and the flame still quavered, but around it was no altar, just a long wooden table with a few papers upon it. A fat man stood by the table, a sword at his side, dressed in a suit of swaggering peacock. Another in black beside him.

While I watched, the peacock man held some sealing wax to the flame and it dropped like blood on to the paper below. He pulled a ring from his plump finger and plunged it into the wax. The man in black stooped and scratched with a quill. His face was pale. He did not speak.

'Bring us the wine, boy. We'll drink to a new life!' The voice was coarse and loud. The voice of a confident bully. Sir Jocelyn, the timeserver.

Then I saw the boy. He came forward with goblets and a pitcher and laid them gently on the table. He did not look at the men but filled both goblets and drew back into the shadows while the toast was drunk.

I don't remember the music. I don't remember finishing the carol. All I can remember is moving to the edge of the balustrade, wary as a cat, in case the dream vanished and I never saw him again.

The two men walked slowly through the door behind the table. Sir Jocelyn laid a genial arm on the bent shoulders of the other man, slapping him on the back.

For a moment Adam stood there, pitcher in hand, looking at the table. Then he turned to follow his father. I knew he was going for ever.

'Adam,' I called, running at full tilt down the spiral staircase.

'Adam, I could not tell him!'

I saw him pause and look at me. Then the world went black.

Sixteen

Goodbye Cloud Cuckoo Land

WELL, THAT'S IT. That brings everything up to date—December 28th to be exact. I missed my Christmas dinner, I broke my leg falling down the staircase, I never found the priest's hole and I never reached Adam. I failed all round. Perhaps I imagined the whole thing, but I'll never know now because it is all over.

Even if it happened, Adam is not at Belvedere now. I cannot go up to the pavilion, even when I have managed to get pretty nimble on these crutches. Oh yes and one more thing. I am not even in the rose room, but in the Infirmary, so I am not even sure if the pattern of the roses was true. I wanted it to be different so much, but now I know I'll never see Adam again.

The only thing that haunts and haunts me is this. Did Father Gerard manage to get away, or was he caught and thrown into prison?

29th December
Father Lewis came to see me this afternoon. He kept looking at me in a worried way. It was obvious that I must have seemed pretty peculiar in the Chapel on Christmas morning. Perhaps they all heard me shouting. I don't know and I haven't asked. It's rather embarrassing really to

have to ask people what you were doing last week. I mean, I ought to be able to remember for myself, that is if I'm not loony.

We had a chat, Father Lewis and I. I think he really wanted me to unburden my soul, but I kept it tightly buttoned up. I did not mention this notebook either, but shoved it under the bedclothes. So we chatted about nothings, broken legs, India, Belvedere, priest holes. Gradually I managed to steer the conversation round to the question that hammers and hammers in my head as I lie staring at the ceiling having restless rests. 'Did he get away?' Only I did not put it like that of course.

'Was Father Gerard ever captured?' I asked casually and almost stopped breathing while waiting for the reply.

'I'm afraid so,' said Father Lewis. 'They got him in the end.'

The room swayed round me and a roaring noise filled my ears. I think I must have fainted because the next thing I remember Sister Anne was there and Father Lewis was looking like a worried spaniel.

'I must have overtired her, Sister.'

'No you didn't.' I shook my head to clear it. 'When was he captured?' I managed to call, as he tiptoed towards the door.

Father Lewis paused. He and Sister Anne exchanged significant looks. The child is off her onion. That sort.

'In the summer of 1594 they caught him near Oxford and put him in the Tower. But he escaped three years later, swung across the moat and got over the wall on a rope. One of the few people ever to escape from the Tower of London.'

'Thank goodness for that!'

I flopped on the pillows, bowled over by relief. Two warm and salty tears trickled joyously down my cheeks. Over and over in my head I said 'He got away!'

Whether it was my warning shout, or whether he worked it out for himself when midnight Mass went wrong, or whether Adam heard me and helped him, it does not matter. The only important thing is that I nearly let Adam down, but it was all right in the end. They never caught him that Christmas long ago.

From now on, I don't have that to worry about. I only have to worry about whether or not it really happened.

New Year's Eve

A day for thinking about New Year resolutions. There is something very sad I have to record. I have worked it all out and it never happened. It was like this. Dad came in and read all that I had written. He took the book away with him to the pub where he is staying. He said he liked something sensational to read in the bath. The next morning he came in and I hardly dared look at him, afraid to know what he thought.

'Beth,' he said gently, 'I know you are wondering if it was all true or not.'

I nodded.

'Well, there is a way you can find out.'

'By looking up records about Sir Jocelyn etc?' I asked.

He shook his head. 'No, that's no good. You

know half of that from the pageant and half from all Father Lewis told you about this place in Elizabethan times.'

He held my hand and curled the fingers slowly one by one. I think he was afraid to go on.

'You say that Adam gave you a silver cross and chain,' he said quietly. 'Well, if you still have the cross and chain, then it is all true.'

I felt round my neck. Nothing. I leaned over and scrabbled wildly in the drawers of the metal bedside locker. Not there either, nor in my suitcase.

'Perhaps it is in the rose room,' I said and my voice went wobbly. Dad shook his head.

'I checked on my way up here.'

I lay back and closed my eyes. It was not true. My stomach hurtled into a bottomless pit, down and down.

'Never mind, honey,' I heard Dad say. 'It was a beautiful dream.'

A beautiful dream. That was all. It was not enough. Last night I lay awake listening to the clock striking the quarter hours. I decided never ever again to imagine things. No more day-dreams, fantasies, moonlit gallops with highway-men, deathbed scenes, castles in the air, surfing away the maths lessons on giant rollers in the Pacific. From now on I will be the sort of person that makes everyone say:

'Beth Lorimer is such a *sensible* child,' and they will all rely on me. Goodbye Cloud Cuckoo Land. I was happy there.

Postcript

New Year's Day

DAD HAD COME AGAIN and we were having tea. I had just hopped on crutches the whole length of the Chapel passage and will obviously soon be ready for a one-legged race. But inside me was this sadness. Sadness about Adam. I still missed him. But I was keeping my New Year resolutions.

Then at tea time, in comes Sister Anne with a boring-looking brown envelope addressed to me and marked 'On Her Majesty's Service.'

'I forgot to give this to you before.'

I tore it open, wondering what Her Majesty required of me. It was from the Sister in the Casualty Ward at the hospital. A little note.

'We took this off when you had your operation.'

I unpacked the tissue paper and there it lay. The silver cross and chain.

I looked at Dad. For once I was lost for words.